A Man Named
BUDD

A Man Named
BUDD

LIFE AND TIMES
OF
HOWARD MALVERN "BUDD" POST,
FOUNDER PBS&J CORPORATION

As Told to Judith Kolva, Ph.D.

authorHOUSE®

AuthorHouse™
1663 Liberty Drive
Bloomington, IN 47403
www.authorhouse.com
Phone: 1-800-839-8640

Published by AuthorHouse 10/15/2014

ISBN: 978-1-4969-4293-7 (sc)
ISBN: 978-1-4969-4292-0 (hc)
ISBN: 978-1-4969-4291-3 (e)

Library of Congress Control Number: 2014917434

Writer, Editor:
Judith Kolva, Ph.D.
Legacies In Ink, LLC
Legaciesink.com
Judith@LegaciesInk.com
954-759-4531

Researcher:
Charles J. Schwabe
Legacies In Ink, LLC
legaciesink.com
Charles@LegaciesInk.com
954-759-4531

Photographs courtesy of the Post family.

Permissions: "Time Is Running Out for Conservation Plan," Florida Keys Reporter, June 15, 1986, Permission granted by Larry Kahn-Editor, The Keynoter, on April 27, 2014.

"Faithless! 'The Girl He Left Behind Him—and His New Girl Over There,'" International News Service, December 22, 1917, Public Domain.

Contents

Contributors

A heartfelt thank you to those who contributed to *A Man Named Budd*:

Jeanne Post: Budd's wife

James Howard "Jimmy" Post: Budd's son

Bob Schuh: Budd's friend and PBS&J partner

Alex Jernigan: Budd's friend and PBS&J partner

Bob Harris: Budd's fellow soldier and PBS&J trusted employee

Bob Toski: Golf swing guru and Budd's friend

Bob Graham: Former U.S. Senator and Florida Governor and Senator

Danny Kolhage: Mayor Pro Tem, 2014, Monroe County

Dedication

This book is dedicated to Jeanne Hendrix Post,

wife, partner, and best friend

of the man named Budd.

Foundations are best when built in solid rock.

Mom is the solid rock of this family.

I LOVE YOU!

Jimmy

Foreword

To those of us with the good fortune to know the man named Budd, I hope this book gives you greater insight into who he was and what made him so special. To the people whom he never met, but were, and still are, affected on a daily basis by him, I hope this book inspires you to be the best you can be.

When it came to life accomplishments, Budd was not one to share. I myself am quite amazed with what I learned from this book, as I never had the courage to read his diaries, which he wrote faithfully from 1936 to January 1, 1998. Thank you, Judith Kolva and Chuck Schwabe, for bringing them to life.

A Man Named Budd is an amazing insight into the "Golden Age" of American life. Through it, Budd in his short, to-the-point way, gives us a great map to happiness and success. To that I, and I am sure many, many others, are eternally grateful.

Thank you, Dad!

I LOVE YOU!

Jimmy

1.

Budd, With *Two* Ds

There wasn't anything special about Oradell. Like all New Jersey boroughs, it was small. Tidy. People were friendly. Hotel Delford was built in 1870, after the Hackensack and New York Railroad's first locomotive steamed through town. Public officials hauled in a 20-foot suction dredge and reengineered the Department of Public-Works' first attempt to dig a reservoir with a clam shell bucket. By 1923, a 22-foot-high concrete dam directed the stony ground Hackensack River into the Oradell Reservoir— an engineering feat that assured pure water for Oradell's citizens. Winters were cold. Slushy. Summers were hot. Humid. All normal. Not special.

Oradell had but three claims to distinction. The first was the giant ginkgo tree on Kinderkamack Road. As the story goes, the Cooper family purchased the then tiny tree from a sea captain who transported it all the way from the Orient.

The second was Soldier Hill, where in 1780, just days before discovering General Benedict Arnold's treason, Major General Lafayette camped, during the Continental Army's foray between Englewood and Jersey City.

The American Revolutionary War was a long battle—eight years, four months, two weeks, one day. Reported casualty figures are probably too low. Yet, records note that 25,000 revolutionaries died in combat and another 25,000 perished from small pox, starving, freezing to death, or rotting on British prison ships. America spent over $150 million— all subsidized by loans and paper money "not worth a continental." Still, this war earned America's independence and Oradell's bragging rights to Soldier Hill.

Oradell's third claim to distinction began on August 25, 1924—a Monday, to be exact. On this day in history, three years after their March 5, 1921 wedding day, 30-year-old Harry Eugene Post and 26-year-old Imogene Areson Nichols Post became parents. From the moment he took his first breath, their son and only child, Howard Malvern Post, was special. *Very* special.

Budd's parents, 1926

No one remembers why. But from childhood, Howard was called *Budd*. And that's Budd, with *two* Ds. Budd, with *two* Ds loved to be asked, "So, why do you call yourself *Budd*?" He would grin and say, "Because, like the beer, I'm *wiser*."

Up and Running

Budd was an obedient little boy. Handsome. Longish, thick blonde hair. Brown eyes. He liked school. From the first day of kindergarten through graduate school, he was an excellent student. Budd's mother (family and friends called her *Jean)* was a stay-at-home mom. Harry was an accountant. The Post family was happy. Comfortable.

King of Westwood, New Jersey, at five years old

After all, this was the Roaring Twenties. World War I—*the war to end all wars*—was over. The United States of America returned to business. With Republicans in the White House, the country prospered . . .

America's population boomed to seven million. Life expectancy reached an all-time high: fifty-four years. The Dow Jones soared to 100 points. Unemployment was five percent. Average annual earnings reached $1,236. Wonder Bread sold for 9¢ a loaf, Maxwell House coffee 47¢ a pound, Wheaties—*The Breakfast of Champions*—10¢ a box, Hostess Cakes 25¢ a package, Baby Ruth candy bars 5¢ each.

Ignoring American's cries to "get a horse," Henry Ford increased the efficiency of his assembly lines and dropped the price of a new Model T—*the horseless carriage*—to

$320. Gas to fuel it cost 18¢ a gallon. Just introduced red, yellow, and green electric traffic signals, complete with warning buzzers, controlled it. The nation's 387,000 miles of freshly paved roadways allowed adventure-seekers to drive from California to New York in 13 days.

Harry, Imogene, and Budd

Technology turned the era upside down . . . electric irons, pop-up toasters, refrigerators, vacuum cleaners, home hair dryers, electric shavers, and rotary dial telephones made life easy. Radios and talking movies made life fun. Almost better, the general public could purchase "the good life" on credit.

Not to be left behind, the medical field introduced major breakthroughs . . . Vitamins, sulfa drugs, penicillin, insulin, the electrocardiogram, TB vaccinations, and an immunization for scarlet fever increased life expectancy.

Convention and Victorian morality were tossed aside. A new woman shocked the nation. She was a flapper. She bobbed her hair, wore make-up, shucked her corset, and showed off short skirts. She smoked, drank, and shimmied to the Charleston. She, according to her newly liberated sisters, was the *bee's knees*. After all, this was the first time in history she was allowed to vote.

In America's ballparks, fans began a love affair with baseball. Babe Ruth—*The Sultan of Swat*—was their hero. In America's nightclubs, the jazz culture took on a beat of its own—Duke Ellington, Louis Armstrong, Count Basie, Ella Fitzgerald made musical improvisation mainstream.

Charles Lindberg—*Lucky Lindy*—completed the first solo flight across the Atlantic Ocean. The first motor hotel—*Motel Inn*—opened in California. Macy's hosted the first Thanksgiving Day parade. MGM's lion roared on the big screen.

Clarence Birdseye, a naturalist from New York, invented frozen food. Accountant, Walter Diemer, concocted pink Double Bubble gum. A California entrepreneur by the name of Roy Allen sold the first frosty mug of A&W root beer for a nickel. White Castle opened the first fast food hamburger chain and sold small, square sliders for five cents. Kimberly-Clark announced Kleenex. Johnson & Johnson introduced the Band-Aid. But in the hearts of many Americans, Edwin Perkins of Omaha, Nebraska, created the most important invention of the era (if not all-time)—Kool-Aid.

On a macro-level, America's economy boomed. Banks loaned money. *Lots* of money. Borrowers spent two out of every five advanced dollars to buy stocks. On September 3, 1929, the stock market peaked. Economist Irving Fisher announced, "Stock prices have reached what looks like a permanent plateau."

On a micro-level, the Post family liked New Jersey. Harry liked his job. Jean liked their house. Budd liked school. He had friends who liked doing what little boys do—shoot marbles, ride bikes, climb trees, play in the park. Life in the Post household was good. Optimistic. Abundant. Even exuberant.

9 Clinton Ave. Westwood N.J

Budd's birth place

Then, on October 24, 1929—*Black Thursday*—the Dow lost 11 percent of its value, at opening bell. Chaos.

On October 28—*Black Monday*—the slide continued. By closing bell, the Dow lost another 13 percent. So many shares changed hands brokers could not record them all. More chaos.

On October 29—*Black Tuesday*—shouts of, "SELL! SELL! SELL!" drowned out the market's opening bell. Brokers made margin calls. Phone lines clogged. Western Union telegrams tripled in volume. Trader fistfights broke out. Investors' life savings were wiped out in a heartbeat.

By the time the market closed, more than sixteen million shares changed hands. Fifteen thousand miles of ticker tape lay curled on the trading floor. The Dow lost yet another 12 percent—over $30 billion in three days. *Beyond* chaos.

Along with the rest of the country, the Dow slid swiftly, steadily, solidly into the Great Depression. By year-end 1932, 13 million Americans (25 percent) were unemployed. They picked up whatever money they could—a little here, a little there. Every little bit counted. It all helped fill the common pot.

Fourteen million people lived in unheated, unsanitary, overcrowded tenements. Thousands less fortunate were forced out onto the streets. Banks closed. Factory doors were nailed shut. Mobs scrounged dirty city markets for scraps of spoiled food. Kellogg's Bran Flakes cost 10¢ a box, eggs 15¢ a dozen, and bacon 19¢ a pound. But pockets were empty. Folks stood in bread lines and flocked to soup kitchens.

Families that could afford milk toast, oatmeal mixed with lard, boiled cabbage, chicken feet simmered in water, or white bread sandwiches made with *only* ketchup, mayonnaise, lard, or potato peels were well off. Families that ate Spam and noodles mixed with cream of mushroom soup were rich.

The mantra of the masses was: *Repair. Reuse. Make do. Never throw anything away.* Mothers mended socks and sewed patches over knee-holes. New dresses, pants, and even underwear were fashioned from patterned feed and flour sacks. Younger children wore hand-me-downs.

Hobos rode the rails and begged for food at farmhouses. Bandits raided highways. Men who could no longer provide for their families pulled the trigger. Parents packed up children, veiled their pride, and moved in with extended family.

It was the Dark Ages all over again.

2.

Alligators and Avocados

Harry was a hard worker. Driven. He managed to hold on to his accountant's job until early 1935. But when his company went belly-up, he decided to move his wife and son to Miami Springs, Florida, where at least winters were warmer.

Harry had two possessions . . . an old Model A Ford and a new hundred-dollar bill. He situated Jean and Budd in the Model A, stuffed the bill in his pocket, and drove south out of Jersey, hoping for a better life.

Interstate highways were yet to be built. Roads were constructed from rock, sand, or even shells. But the model A—Henry Ford's new *Baby Lincoln*—was a "miracle." Sporty. Jaunty. Sparkling. It came in four colors—tan, deep blue, olive green, maroon—each with shiny black fenders. The 3-speed gear-box required the driver to double-clutch, but no one complained. After all, it had "remarkable acceleration," cruised at forty miles an hour, and reached a top speed of fifty-five, maybe even sixty-five, miles an hour.

No one knows where the Post family stayed along the way or how they managed basic creature comforts. Uncharacteristically, Budd did not record or relay *any* details.

Jimmy says . . .

> *The only thing Dad said about their trip from Jersey to Florida was how long it took—three months, to drive just over a thousand miles, down parts of U.S. 1 and A1A, in that Model A Ford. It was brutal.*

We do know Harry rented an apartment, on NW 36 Street, across from Miami Jackson High School, in the Allapattah neighborhood, within the City of Miami. Allapattah was founded in 1856, when William P. Wagner, the earliest permanent "white" citizen, arrived from Charleston, South Carolina.

Mr. Wagner established a homestead on a hammock alongside Miami Rock Ridge and borrowed the Seminole Indian word meaning *alligator* to name his new home. It seemed appropriate. After all, during the 1800s, alligators and avocados were neighbors.

When the Post family arrived in 1934, Allapattah was predominately a "white" neighborhood. Folks were friendly. Neighborly. Palm trees lined streets. No one thought twice about walking downtown. (When it rained, Jean spent a dime and rode the bus.) *Crime* was but a word in the dictionary.

Allapattah was a typical 1930s small town. The five-and-dime store, with its metal cash register, candy counter, and creaky wooden floor, sold brooms, dustpans, tin pepper boxes, gravy strainers, biscuit cutters, flour dredges, egg whips, apple corers, pie plates, tack hammers, boot blacking, baseballs, pencil charms, lined writing tablets, shaving brushes, jewelry (mostly red), candle sticks, handkerchiefs, needles, thread, even police whistles. Most gadgets cost a nickel—maybe a dime. Expensive items, though, sold for 20¢.

The Live and Let Live Drugstore's large display windows were trimmed with crepe paper. Ailing customers could buy everything from Ex-Lax, Mercurochrome, and Sloan's Liniment, to mustard plaster and toothache remedies. Lucky Strike and Old Gold cigarettes cost a quarter, for two packs. King Edward *el cheapo* cigars cost a nickel, for two. Premium Perfecto Garcia cigars cost a quarter, for two. The step-on, black and white, "guaranteed accurate weight" Toledo scale was free.

The Double Kay Nut Machine, heated by two large light bulbs, was filled with fresh, warm peanuts, cashews, and mixed nuts. A magazine rack stood next to it. Everybody liked *Life* and *Look*. Men bought *Gangster* and *Popular Science*. Women snuck in for *True Confessions*. Kids sat on the floor and read *Batman, Robin, Superman*, and *Wonder Woman* comics.

Wall cases displayed cosmetics—Coty lipstick and Armand face powder and rouge were especially popular. Gifts were located next to cosmetics. Customers bought Evening in Paris gift sets, wrapped in fancy paper, and Chantilly cologne for women; boxed billfolds for men; Sheaffer pen sets for grads; cups, spoons, and booties for babies. Gift cards cost a quarter.

The pharmacy, where the druggist mixed prescriptions, was a separate room in the back of the store. He shook powders into a pestle, ground them with a mortar, spooned the mixture into small papers, folded the papers in half, and turned up the corners. He typed labels, one at a time.

Then, there was the Allapattah public library, shoe repair shop, funeral home, movie house, Screwball bar, Al's restaurant, jewelry store, and Baptist Church. That was it.

Good old Mom & Dad! Summer of '39

Harry's very first day in Florida was busy. He got up early, grabbed a quick breakfast, and hit the streets, looking for a job. Eight hours later, he opened the door to their apartment and grinned at Jean. "Lost it," Harry said.

"Lost *what*?"

"My hundred-dollar bill."

Well, Harry's hundred-dollar bill was *long gone*. Jean glared. She retreated to the kitchen and stirred her soup. Fast.

Harry followed her. "Lighten up, Jean. I'm the brand new salesman for Miami Stationery Company," he said.

Not an accountant's job, but at least he could earn a living.

Harry was a hard worker. Determined. Driven. Time passed. Harry's accounts grew. His client relationships blossomed.

As so happened, one of Harry's clients—Jackson Memorial Hospital—heard about his accounting background and hired him to work in their accounting department. Eventually, Harry was promoted to head accountant.

But Harry's career path didn't stop in accounting.

Jimmy says . . .

> *My grandfather was a good businessman. As time passed, Jackson Hospital had financial difficulties that included inventory control problems. All kinds of stuff just disappeared. Well, to date, the hospital administrator had been a doctor. But the governing board had enough. They revolted and decided to kick him out. The board needed a business person to run the business side of the hospital, so they promoted my grandfather to be Jackson Memorial Hospital's first non-physician administrator.*

Back in the '30s, that was a *very* big deal.

3.

Nowhere. Nothing.

The Post family lived in their apartment about a year before Harry bought a large lot and contracted with Tommy Tompkins to build a house at 871 Lake Drive in Miami Springs, Florida.

The house was tiny—a conventional 1938 CBS (composite building style) one-story, with a tile roof, three bedrooms, one bath, screened-in porch, detached two-car garage. Its claim to fame was it was the second house built in the western half of Miami Springs.

It's good to be home

The Post property was off South Royal Poinciana Boulevard, across from Deleon Park. It was the largest lot on the lake. Actually, two lakes flowed into the Miami River. Lake Drive split them; a big pipe connected them.

During the '30s, the area was on the edge of the Everglades. It was, basically, nowhere, with nothing around. Still, just north of what was then called *Pan American Field,* the neighborhood was fresh. Growing.

In 1927, Pan American Airways' executives decided to move their base of operations from Key West to Miami. So, they purchased 116 acres along NW 36 Street from the Seminole Fruit and Land Company. When, in 1928, their airport was complete, Pan American Field boasted two hard-surfaced runways and two hangars.

Pan Am's inaugural flight took off September 15, 1928, when Captain Edwin Musick piloted a Sikorsky-38 to Havana via Key West. During its first year of operation, Pan American Field handled around 8,000 passengers and 20 tons of cargo. (During 2012, almost 28 million passengers and two million tons of cargo passed through what was by then called *Miami International Airport—MIA* for short.)

Pan Am's original terminal building (purchase price: fifty grand) was the first passenger facility of its type in the United States. It was a two-story, reinforced concrete structure, with a high-domed ceiling and numerous large windows. Passenger services and amenities were on the lower level. Offices and a balcony, with an impressive view of the airfield, were on the upper level.

Jimmy says . . .

> *My grandparents were trailblazers. Visionaries. Their neighborhood was out in the woods, on the edge of civilization. But I'm confident they believed it would change.*
>
> *The location was perfect for Dad—fishing, swimming, and a park with a baseball field, were a stone's throw away. Eventually, the City of Miami even built Miami Springs Golf and Country Club in the area. Dad loved going to the Everglades. He loved the outdoors, period.*
>
> *Dad also loved guns. Back when he was a kid, everybody had a shotgun. He didn't venture into the Everglades without one—he'd be a darned fool if he did. Huge snakes were everywhere. I have a picture of my grandmother standing in their yard, over a water moccasin, with a shotgun. The snake was deader than a doornail. Grandma was a fiery old broad—not afraid of anything.*
>
> *Dad loved to tell the story about walking to school with his best friend, Art Peavy (PV), one winter morning. They were almost across a field in an old cattle farm, when they spotted an eighteen-foot rattlesnake, bigger around than a man's thigh. Well, good thing it was cold, good thing it was morning, because that snake was frozen and not awake—yet.*

Dad picked it up, wound it around his neck, and let it hang over his arms. Its head draped on the ground on the left side. Its tail draped on the ground on the right side. Those were the days when big snakes were BIG snakes.

Don't mess with Mom!

By late August 1938, the Posts were settled into their new home. Harry worked long hours. But Jean didn't care. She was independent. Busy. And from early on, very involved in the community.

Jimmy says . . .

> *My grandmother started two churches: The First*
> *Methodist Church of Miami Spring, and later, Miami*
> *Springs First Presbyterian Church.*
>
> *But Grandma wasn't by any means a religious*
> *fanatic. She was a go-to-church-on-Sunday kind of*
> *gal. The rest of the week she did her thing—smoked*
> *her cigarettes and drank her liquor.*

Jean's community involvement didn't end with churches.
She started the first women's club in Miami Springs.
Typical of the era, the "little Mrs." was busy being *busy.*

Sunday drive to Homestead

Jean was a chronic collector. (Some suggest *horrendous*
hoarder describes her better.) She saved stamps, stashed
silver coins in Tupperware containers, displayed dog
statues, hung cast iron pans, and showed off blue and white
Wedgewood dishes.

Jean was especially fond of newspaper clippings. She started her collection during World War I. The then 19-year-old Jean, like all young women of the era, longed for—fretted about—their men "over there."

Nell Brinkley expressed their sentiments in a daily International News Service column. Jean saved every one.

For instance . . .

Faithless!

"The Girl He Left Behind Him— and His New Girl 'Over There'"

By Nell Brinkley

December 22, 1917

Eyes of Gray, as gray as the sea "himself" has called upon— gray eyes a glitter with tears as the sky of November was above the troop ship that day, eyes of gray are sober without eyes of brown to come home to. Sure that was a sodden, thick, black day with a crying wind in the sky to weep in the ship's ropes and tweak a body's "bayonet-bow" or a body's new hat, over one eye, to wet cold cheeks with silver mist and to freeze the heart-gone cold already, into a little stone under her jacket.

But just before—just before—after long hours when she could neither run clear away or be close beside him, but stood an eager little figure smiling back at the leaning, gazing one in khaki-tan across the tiny, infinite gulf of green pay water that lay, and ocean, between the transport rail and the pier—just before the bells rang and the great ship sailed, the gray sky wiped the mist from her blue eyes, the sun washed the world in pale splendor of gold and a banner came into the sky, deepening overhead to a blue field fit for the silver stars and fading to the sea-edge in rippling band after band of rose and white.

It was a sign—a good token . . . but WHAT if someone should whisper that already he was faithless? Had found a new girl now? Loved a maid with chestnut hair and soft dark eyes. Courter her by the roadside often and over again—gave her the very chocolates and jam that Gray-eyes sent him over? Called her the very sweet pet names that Gray-eyes taught him?

Then, there was the "diary thing." Jean kept a diary, well, *forever.* And in 1939, it was time to pass the tradition on to her son.

Jeanne says . . .

That Imogene was a strict one—a real spitfire. Fierce. She was petite, about five feet three inches, had red hair, fair skin, and piercing brown eyes. She was abrupt. She told you exactly what she thought, no matter what. And when she looked right through you with those eyes, oh my! She scared me, and everybody else, to death.

She scared Budd too. She laid down the law, and he minded her. Budd never wanted to disappoint Mom. Actually, he didn't DARE disappoint Mom. So when she bought him a diary in 1939 and told him to write, he wrote.

And for the next 59 years, Budd wrote nearly every day.

4.

Brite and Faiя

Before writing, people left palm prints on cave walls. They scratched on rocks. They created complex hieroglyphics. They memorized stories.

Then, around 8,000 BCE, in the fertile, crescent land of Sumner (an ancient Mesopotamian civilization) writing was invented. *Cuneiform*, as the system was called, had over 1,500 distinct, wedge-shaped marks that ancients carved on clay tablets with blunt reeds.

Centuries passed. Eventually, Chinese, Mayans, Egyptians, Greeks, Phoenicians, and, finally, Europeans developed writing systems. Scribes were the first to write regularly . . . exactly . . . willingly. So, common folk recited letters they wanted sent, even stories they wanted preserved to village scribes.

Again, time passed. As paper became more widely available, writing became more commonplace. And with the advance of writing, came diary writing. The word *diary* comes from the Latin *diārium* (daily allowance). Diaries are personal. Frank. Forthright. Poignant.

The first known diary was written, in Greek, during the second half of the second century, by Roman Emperor, Marcus Aurelius. He called it *To Myself* (*Τὰ εἰς ἑαυτόν*).

The first famous diary was written, in Japanese, during the late 10th and 11th centuries, by lady-in-waiting, Sei Shōnagon. She called it *The Pillow Book (枕本)*.

Sei Shōnagon's pillow book—a book that is still read and respected eleven centuries later—preserves her thoughts and observations about the pleasures and perils of nobility in the Heian court of Empress Consort Tesishi. She wrote poetry and described nature. She made almost two hundred lists. She offered advice on etiquette. She taught the refined art of penning love letters. She gossiped. She complained. She even explained, openly, erotic satisfactions derived from "the things that make you nervous."

Sei Shōnagon's diary is a testimonial to the African proverb "When a person dies, a library burns." It's true. When someone departs this earth, their unique experience as a human being is lost. Gone. Usually forgotten. UNLESS . . . unless they leave a diary.

Through her diary, Sei Shōnagon will be remembered. Understood. Respected. Appreciated. Forever.

june 1936

Happy to be in Miami, 1936

And over 1,000 years later, on a continent 7,000 miles distant, so will Howard Malvern (Budd, with *two* Ds) Post.

Budd Post's first diary entry . . .

> Sunday January 1, 1939
>
> "Brite and Faiя"
>
> Good Morning: Went to Sunday school and then came home and fixed Mr. Nelson's gun and PV and I shot away a whole box of slugs.—Sun. had fried chicken & stuff. Mrs. Wilkes and Mrs. Balling ate with us. Miz Balling got here day 'fore

yesterday. Went to league tonight and came home & messed around & then went to bed.

My but I'm a child still here! I am a child ready to reveal ~~~~~~

5.

Resolved and Revised

Some kids are good kids. Some kids are great kids. Some kids are greater kids. Then there was Budd Post. No matter what he did (and even as a kid he did a lot), Budd was the *greatest* kid imaginable.

No one told Budd what to do. He came to this world with an inner force—a determined determination—that drove him to be the best of the best, no matter what.

Budd wrote in his diary . . .

Be the Best

1940 New Year Resolutions . . .

Resolved:

1. No Smoking (Easy)
2. Improve Golf (plenty of room)
3. Regular Church and S. School
4. Read more Good Books
5. Write my Diary well
6. Be a good boy, generally

Revised:

1. More Sunday School & Church
2. Better Golf
3. Don't putt what they give you
4. Be careful in sand traps
5. Always know whether a putt meant anything—don't just "bat" short ones
6. Think before you pick a club & before you hit the shot
7. Be on my toes, generally

Been looking back. I am a sap. I only read <u>96</u> books last year. Rated each one. I'll list the **Good** ones:

1. Disputed Passage—Loyd [sic] C. Douglas
2. Green Light—Loyd [sic] Douglas
3. Horse & buggy—Dr. Hertgler
4. Good Country Lawyer—Bellamy Partridge
5. With Malice Toward None—Herman Morrow
6. It Can't Happen Here—Sinclair Lewis
7. The Doctor—Mary Roberts Reinheart (506 pages)
8. American Years—Harold Sinclair
9. Oh for the Lamps of China—Alice Hobart
10. All This & Heaven too—Rachel Fields
11. Gone with the Wind (twice)
12. Hope Deferred—hope makes the heart sick, but a longing fulfilled is a tree of life
13. Sherlock Holmes—note to self: his theory of observation is a good one to follow. I will do it.

14. All Quiet on the Western Front is indescribable!!!
15. And, of course, the Bible

Best Bible passages are:

1. Ten Commandments—Exodus
2. Benediction—Genesis
3. Hebrews leaving Egypt—Exodus
4. Psalm 43—"Send out Thy Light"
5. Psalm 86
6. Psalm 90
7. Psalm 100
8. Shortest Psalm—117
9. Longest Psalm—119
10. Well known Psalm—121
11. Song of Solomon
12. Assembly Psalm—146
13. David & Goliath
14. Solomon's Wisdom—I Kings, Chap 3
15. Good Bible Story—Esther Chap. 3-8
16. Shortest Chap. except Psalm—Chap. 10 Esther
17. The Lord giveth & he taketh away . . . . Job Chap. I

Good Morning: Oh nuts! Will do better in my future—always, always, will do well. It's like the sermon I heard in church—"Nothing is too good to be true." I ask myself: What do YOU know?—I know something about everything and everything about something. . . . But war . . . war . . . war. I refuse to grow up to be cannon fodder.

Good Nite!!   § § § §

31

In 1898, L. J. Becker donated land at the corner of NW 36 Street and NW 17 Street, in Miami Florida's Allapattah neighborhood. The town built a log cabin and opened a one-room grade school. The first year fourteen students enrolled.

Over the years, the building grew to a four-room grade school, then a nine-room grade school. As Northwest Miami spread from a small town to an urban metropolis, the school continued to expand. By the time Budd enrolled as a freshman in 1938, Andrew Jackson High School—home of the green and gold *Generals*—was a three-story high school.

To say Budd was a good student is trite. Conventional. Budd was an extraordinary student. Even brilliant. When he graduated in June 1942, he had a long list of accomplishments.

- ✓ Scholastic average for three and a half years of high school: 91.75 percent
- ✓ Graduated with 18 credits, 16 being the requirement
- ✓ Eagle Scout
- ✓ President of Andrew Jackson's Key Club
- ✓ Vice President of Andrew Jackson's National Honor Society
- ✓ Secretary of Andrew Jackson's student body
- ✓ Vice President Andrew Jackson's student body
- ✓ Member of Andrew Jackson's glee club

- ✓ Circulation Manager, *Old Hickory,* Andrew Jackson's annual
- ✓ Captain of Andrew Jackson's golf team
- ✓ Varsity golf letter
- ✓ Florida State High School Golf Champion
- ✓ Class Valedictorian
- ✓ American Legion Medal
- ✓ National Rifle Association Junior Diploma—Marksman, Pro-marksman, Marksman—First Class, Sharpshooter
- ✓ Junior Chamber of Commerce award for athletics and scholarship
- ✓ Delegate to State Student Council Convention

Budd's principal acknowledged him as "one of the finest students with whom I have associated."

ANDREW JACKSON HIGH SCHOOL
171 NW 36 Street
Miami, Florida

W. W. Matthews, Principal
James T. Wilson, Supt.

Dade County Schools
Mar. 4, 1943

TO WHOM IT MAY CONCERN:

Howard Post, one of our high school graduates of June, 1942 was in the upper twenty-five percent of his class, both scholastically and in student activities.

In the placement tests given to all seniors of high schools in the state of Florida he ranked among the highest in the state. His scores were as follows: Henman Nelson test, 99; English 94; Social studies, 99; Natural Science, 98; Math, 98. For these tests 50 was median.

During his high school years Howard was very active in the following student leadership groups: Member of the National Honor Society, Key Club President, Student Council, Annual Staff, Golf team all four years, won the State championship in Golf his Senior year.

I am happy to recommend Howard Post as one of the finest students with whom I have been associated during the past few years.

Very truly yours,
Wilber c. Worley
WCW: vk

Look out, world. Here he comes!

Budd wrote in his diary . . .

"Brite and Faiя"

Good Morning—School is getting me down. Damnation!!! (Got to stop using dam, etc. That's all there is to it!!!) Had a Latin vocab. test and didn't know all the principal pasts of some of the verbs. Well, in the end got a good grade on my test—made 100%. Mad at my dam algebra, though. This shit's hard!!

Clyde (Foster) & I won our debate: Resolved: The U.S. and Great Britain should form as military alliance?

Practiced some at the typewriter. I **AM** going to learn to type, on my own.

After my Senior Tests, I am exempt in EVERYTHING!!! Wait a minute. Damned if I didn't win the American Legion medal. Surprised? Well, I should say. Dad gave me five dollars for getting the medal.

School Year 1939-40

Good Morning—What's good about it?! My diary is a day late because I was sick. Anyway, up and at 'em at usual time. Ate and off to catch school bus. Worked in library this afternoon as usual. (Am reading "Life on the Mississippi" by Mark Twain.) Like the library a lot. Got new desk.

It sure is a honey. Came home and read Abe Lincoln in Illinois and Chapter 3 of Kings—Abe is quite a play. Started reading "Conservation of our Natural Resources." Very Good!!!

Student Council 6th period & minutes are all written. Officers of Student Council were installed. When Pres. Bob Hubach swore me in as secretary he said sromise & pware instead promise & sware. Sec'y is usually a hard job.

Got 100% on the history test. Latin is easy now. Here's what I'll do for homework tonite. I'm determined to finish!!!

1. Butterfly classifications
2. Drawings of Body
3. Latin verbs
4. Geometry—Dad is pretty good in Geometry. So am I!!!
5. Then, read Bible—Kings thru. Chap. 15

Got report card today: Geometry 80% even with a 60% grade on monthly test—**Dam!** Won't happen again!!!—Latin only 92%, English 95%, Biology 96%, History 98%.

Went to dentist and now I'm finished for a while (have 27 teeth & 1/3 are filled). Incidentally, I received a medal for my citizenship essays.

PV is my best friend. Hot dog!

Budd and PV soaking it up

Then in April 1941, tragedy struck the Post family.

Budd wrote in his diary . . .

<u>April 3, 1941</u>

> Good Morning—**MAN!!** What a day!! Dad left this am on 7:30 plane with Mrs. Allen. I took his car to school and school went OK. After 2:30 I went downtown—got a shine at Milby's and started up the street. At Miami Ave. and Flagler a boy was hollering "16 Missing in E.A.L. Plane." Damn!!!
>
> I bought a paper & it <u>was</u> Dad's plane. I <u>tore out</u> to home (85-90 at times) and spent couple hours in terrible suspense. Finally Mrs. Huffstutter called & said plane was found and everybody was safe.

Man it was terrific. Mom passed out—neighbors etc. streamed in & out—Mr. Lassiter called & boy oh boy! It's one mess. We're waiting for Dad to call now.

April 4, 1941

Good Morning—Boy what a day. We waited for Dad to call but finally realized he wasn't going to call. Bungle, Bob & I started to go up there about 7:30 but Uncle Charley, Howard etc. talked us out of it. Dam.

I finally went to bed about 11:00. About 11:01 they woke me up and Uncle Charley, Howard, Bob, & I left for Vero Beach hospital. We learned Dad was at Fort Pierce so we went back. Saw his room but he was asleep. We came back—got back about 7:45. I ate a little bite of breakfast and then went down to school. Honor society tapped. I made it!!

April 5, 1941

Good Morning: I saw Dad and talked to him for a few minutes. I had a Coke just a few minutes before I saw him—when I saw him after a few minutes my stomach started to go & I went black—managed to walk out and after a second was OK again. We turned right around and came home. I drove more than half way.

Got home about 2:30. We're having some squall now—raining and blowing cats & dogs outside. After reading papers telling about crash went

39

downtown. Got "shot" at Dr's and did a couple of other things. Then over to Biltmore. Played back nine for 7 holes. I bought a pair of shoe trees for my new golf shoes which I just got today. Mom called and said Dad was getting along pretty well.

April 11, 1941

Good Morning: I left house at 7:30 and we were down at Long Bridge and unloaded by 9:30. Rented a boat (#13) We had already put 13 gals. of gas in car and started out. Motor was punk but put a little oil in & Oh Boy! Fellow who rented the boat pointed out Pumpkin Key but we followed the chart. Went to Angelfish creek and a couple of big creeks north PV and I caught 1 grunt and that was our total catch. Got home in house at exactly 5:10 but Mom exploded. Nobody knows where we've been. Saw Dad about six—he's in pain—back and leg—going to operate tomorrow. I continue to read news of the crash. Even though Dad had a broken leg he stayed in the plane and let others be rescued before him. Very brave!!!

May 1, 1941

Dad in lots of pain. Was up all nite. A Dr. came out—a rectum specialist—and gave Dad an enema etc.—really hurt 'cause Dad broke down & cried. Damn PUNK!!! Wonder what will happen to dad.

Budd never connected the dots. We, too, are left wondering. Budd's last diary entries for 1941 and 1942 are about his experiences at Andrew Jackson High School . . .

School year 1941-1942

> Finished organizing my schedule today—I hope. I'm taking English, Latin, Chemistry, Solid Geometry, American History. That's all. Have them all in the morning so have two S.H. in the afternoon.

> Remember my New Year's Resolutions!!! Especially, stop being SAP. Show what I can do. Got Dale Carnegies book "How to Win Friends and Influence People." Read it. DO it.

> THINK!!! Went out to Palma Ceia Golf Course. After lunch at hotel I met Mr. Bosarg. Guess I'll get into West Point after all!!

> Sold annuals from 11:30 till three. Annual is SWELL. Stayed after school with a gang signing annuals. Incidentally, I was elected President of the Key Club today and received award for Key Club Hall of Fame. My mind is full of thoughts of things to do, mostly concerning Riflery, Golf, & the Keys. Then, there is Pearl Harbor. After supper read "Plan for Conquest" by Joe Harsch. GOOD!!! Remember your resolutions!!! Plus your attitude!!

> Had assembly 3rd period—Boy!! I almost dropped dead when I won the Junior Chamber of Commerce award for athletics and scholarship. Practiced my speech [valedictorian] for graduation and messed

around. Went over to golf course and played six holes then Hugh came out and we started to prepare for the dance. Finally, hurried home & got down to school about 7:50. Graduation was OK—my speech wasn't so hot—<u>says Dad</u>. After graduation went out to C.C. for dance. Dance was kinda punk.

Good Morning—up at about 7:20 and off to school via school bus for last time. That's it.

I reported to Civil Service Commission and to take examination for Pepper's appointment to West Point. Exam took from 8:30 to 3:00 to finish it all—Six exams, Algebra, Geometry, Literature, English, Ancient & American History. Here's hopin!!! Came home and read "Sun is My Undoing." Excellent, excellent historical fiction!! Must get ready to report to Marion Military School.

Wonder where I'll be and what I'll be doing one year from today.

Good Nite from Jackson High!!

Some suggest boys and girls are the epitome of yin and yang—two opposites bound together, separate, yet fused. How two seemingly incompatible forces can create harmony may remain one of life's unsolved mysteries.

Jimmy says . . .

I can't say for certain, because Dad didn't talk about it. Still, based on what he accomplished in high school, my guess is he was popular. It's also a good guess that he did well in the "girl department."

Based on pictures, I can tell you, for sure, after the war, Dad dated good-looking women from powerbroker families in South Florida. After all, Dad was a very smart man—never one to get stuck, anywhere, any time.

Yet, his life with girls wasn't always, shall we say, "easy"? Nonetheless, Dad was determined. Once he made his mind up, there was no stopping him—whatever the situation.

Budd wrote in his diary . . .

"Brite & Faiя—Faiя to Middlin"

Oh Gosh. Read one of dad's old love letters to Mom & nearly <u>died</u>. **WOW**.

Am going to try to get my light-o-love (her name is Carrie) to go to the benefit show at the Federal tomorrow nite. Here's hopin! . . . Went to theatre and saw the Emperor's New Clothes. Excellent!!!! Carrie was in blue & Oh Boy is she cute!!!!

Phooey. Carrie won't go to the show with me again. Will try again tomorrow. Most important thing of the day is that Carrie's sore at me. Don't blame her because I stood her up on the boat ride. Mom's fault. Wouldn't let me go. Dam it! . . . Dam it! Wish Carrie wasn't mad at me.

Went downtown today and met Carrie (thrill, thrill). Ate lunch with her (XOX). Will kiss her tomorrow so help me (I hope). Leave for St. Pete tomorrow. Will give Carrie a good luck charm. Will try to kiss her good bye.

KISSED Carrie good bye. Oh boy!!!!

Carrie won't go to the show with me. Paul is trying hard for Carrie. He is welcome to her!

WOW! What a party. Kissed Belle plenty. Boy what a day!!!

HURRAY!!! WE BEAT EDISON!!! 7-0/!!! Boy, I'm so happy I could _____. Then Belle went with some boy from Edison. Boy did they look sick! And of all things they sat rite behind us!!! Oh, well. Such is life. Next!!

Went to card party. Had good time. PV & I snitched some ice cream. Shame on us! Isy was there and she sure looked cute in red and white. Oh well. It took me about an hour to screw up courage, but I got a date with Virginia for tomorrow nite. Going to see Olivia DeHaviland in "My Love Came Back." Hot dog!!!

Girls PHOEY! I love 'em. I hate 'em. It's been a strange year [1942]. I've been growing up so fast. The world's a mess but it will be worse not better.

My prayer for the New Year—Peace on Earth—
Good Will to **Men**!!!

——⁓⁓⁓∘⊙⊰⊙⊙⊱⊙∘⁓⁓⁓——

On April 9, 1939, Budd became an official member of the First Methodist Church of Miami Springs. And for the rest of his life, he was devout. Dedicated. Determined to be a good Christian.

Budd wrote in his diary . . .

> Am going to start to read the Bible all the way through. I'm giving up cokes for Lent. Am also giving up candy. Read through book of Gen. Makes me feel good!!!! It is my Christian duty to be good and read at least one complete chapter of Bible every nite before I go to bed—even if I don't have time to clean my teeth.
>
> Went to church with Mom this morning. Pretty good sermon. Came home, ate, and listened to radio. Then drew this note for the coming week:
>
> **"T-I-T-H-E."** Must put $2.00 in collection plate every Sunday. Or else!!! Checked bank balance—$75. I will do it!!
>
> I really think a lot of them (Mom & Dad) but I think they could be better Christians. I don't hardly ever say anything about them in here. Gee, I don't appreciate how lucky I am, in more ways than one. Still, came home tonite and mom acting like a dam picklepuss. I'll still read the

Bible—Am going to take a bath and go to bed early to read three Chapters of II Chronicles—better than that—I will <u>finish</u> the Book of Second Chronicles.

Good Morning—up and at 'em at eight o'clock. Read funnies and ate. Took a shower and then off to church. Was communion Sunday. Fell from Grace a little this morning, but God willing, I'll improve.

Better now. I was a "Wise Man" in Christmas pageant. Good for me!!! Guess I'll even buy Christmas gifts . . .

Name	Gift	Approx. Price
Mom	Perfume	$1.10
	Candy	$2.50
	House chimes	???
	Stockings	$4.00
	Handkerchiefs	$2.00
	2 White bags	$5.00
	Slippers	$3.00
	Weathervane	???
Dad	Wallet	$7.50
	Socks	$3.00
	1 doz. golf balls	$7.50
	Box cigars	$3.00
	Carton cig.	???

War is HELL!!! & And that G.D.SB. Hitler!!! Hitler is a man damned by God and the world. His time will come. Kick out the dam **Hitler-ism!!** God bless the whole world.

From the get-go, Budd enjoyed sports. From the get-go, Budd wanted to win. From the get-go, Budd won. But if he didn't, *oh my.*

Budd wrote in his diary . . .

> Played tennis with dad for an hour. Did I get mad!!! ##@@*** Score 0-6—6-3—2-2
>
> Bowled at the Stadium Alleys for about hour & half. Was high man first game with 144 for using big ball for first time in life!!! Second game rolled only 123. D_____N!!!
>
> Won 25¢ from Mom—15¢ for wiggling my arms 500 times and 10¢ for letting her read my diary. She's all right and so is dad even if I don't always realize it.
>
> Played tennis with PV. Let him beat me three sets to one even after I had him 5-2 & 5-3 in two sets. <u>DURN!!!</u>
>
> Played ping pong this afternoon. Dam near didn't win. That's 'cause it rained—really rained—all day
>
> and I feel **punk**! Also had headache all day from too much chloroform preparing my bug collection.
>
> Boy, what a day! Golf, Basketball, Swimming, & horseback riding! PV and I went over to Hialeah and played a little basketball. Came back & went swimming. Then went riding. I rode Gold Bug. Best horse I've ever ridden. Peppy! Gosh! Outrode PV all to hell and back.

Love my football. Played this afternoon. Will be as sore as the dickens tomorrow. Who cares!!! I am drinking all the milk and cream possible to gain weight so I can play better. Got milkshake after supper. Marshmallows too. Here's hopin!

Miami U 19 to 0 over Texas Tech and boy am I going to tell PV off for keeping us home!!! Gee, I'm timid!!! **HA!!** I'm ticked!!! Good nite—no Bible—didn't clean teeth—Damnation!!!

Empirical evidence does not corroborate that *collecting* is a link on one's DNA chain. Still, like mother, like son, Budd was a consummate collector. In 1936, he started a stamp collection. Around the same time, he started a newspaper article collection. "Big" headlines interested him.

It was almost as if Budd assembled his collections to make a museum archivist's life easy. Everything—*everything*—was organized meticulously and labeled with Budd's perfect, precise penmanship.

Budd wrote in his diary . . .

Good morning—up and at 'em as usual.

Spend most of the morning catching flutterbys. Caught three new ones today. Got a swallowtail in perfect condition. Turned my bugs into Mr. Roberts. Messed around this aft. & got more chloroform & net. Am going to make a butterfly collection. Got off lite in today's homework. Came home as usual and collected the rest of my bugs. Also collecting leaves.

Asked Mom to help me keep newspaper clippings. A red letter day as a black one—the Pope died today. I've got the clippings. I will keep <u>ALL</u> important clippings.

———〜〜◦◦◦◦◦〜〜———

Then, there was photography. Harry bought his son a camera in 1939, and for the rest of his life, photography was one of Budd's passions. Skills. Accomplishments.

A rare event: Budd on the other end of the camera

Jimmy says . . .

I can tell you, firsthand, Dad always had a camera. But, then, taking pictures is a family thing. I have an album full of pictures from when the family lived in Jersey that go back to the early 1900s.

I remember Dad's Pentax thirty-five millimeter SLR. It cost lots of money, but his camera was one thing Dad splurged on. He absolutely loved taking pictures. I still have cigar box, after cigar box full of his pictures, and like his diaries, each one is labeled with the year.

They are those black-and-white pictures, with the curly white border, that he had to take to the drugstore to get developed. Dad recorded meticulously the year, location, and who was in the picture. But his details didn't stop there. If, say, the picture was of someone catching a big bass, he even wrote how much the fish weighed.

Then, there were the pictures he took during the Korean War . . . P-51 Mustang fighter pilots were dropping bombs. American troops were shooting Browning Automatic Rifles at North Koreans, two hundred yards out. North Koreans were firing back.

And Dad? He wasn't shooting a rifle. He was shooting a camera. Now, that's a guy who loved to take pictures!

Budd wrote in his diary . . .

Camera I want costs fifteen dollars. This morning saw two rabbits eating grass at water's edge. Wish I had camera!

Got my camera for $15. It is loaded and ready to go. Haven't taken any pictures yet—will try tomorrow. Dad paid for camera. Wish I had a lot of money.

Went to town & got my camera case at Simpson's. $4.50. Got my first roll of film back from Burdines. Only 11 out of 18 were any good. Damnation!!! But don't worry. I'll get better.

Went to town. Stopped at bank withdrew money to buy film: $3.00 + $5.40 + $.15 = $8.55. Car is running punk, but went to Biltmore and played with Ned E. and Capt. Jack John. Won $5.00. Had 45-37. After supper Dad suggested I look at Dr. Stephenson's movie equipment (the whole works $100). Good buy—I'll do it.

Went over to bicycle shop and brilliantly let myself get screwed out of $4.50. Traded my bike and $4.50 for a $20 camera.

PUNK. **But I got my camera!!!!**

6.

Prepared. For Life.

In 1946, just shy of his twelfth birthday, Budd raised his right hand and pledged,

"On my honor, I, Howard M. Post, will do my best, to do my duty, to God and my country, and to obey the Scout Law, to help other people at all times, to keep myself physically strong, mentally awake, and morally straight."

And for the rest of his life, Budd upheld the law of the Boy Scouts of America. He was, indeed, brave, cheerful, clean, courteous, friendly, helpful, kind, loyal, obedient, reverent, trustworthy, thrifty—the perfect scout.

Bob Schuh says . . .

> *Budd and I started out together as Boy Scouts, when we were about twelve years old. We were Troop 34. Our meeting place was a church down on Thirty-Sixth Street in Buena Vista, which was Northeast Miami.*
>
> *I lived about a mile north of the church; Budd lived about a mile west, just a couple blocks*

away from a large park called Moore Park. Well, Moore Park had a ball field, so almost every Saturday morning we met at the park and, along with a number of other boys, played a pick-up game of softball before our patrol meeting.

Each Boy Scout troop had about six patrols, consisting of eight, maybe ten, boys each. Our patrol was Beaver Patrol. Over the years, Budd and I argued about which one of us was really the patrol leader. I must tell you the argument was never resolved. But we had fun—lots of fun.

A good part of what scout leaders preach is about how to be good boys who grow to good men. You know—loyal, trustworthy, honest, brave. Those qualities are good for everyone. We may have turned out all right anyway, but I do believe Boy Scouts helped us character wise.

Then, we learned the usual skills Boy Scouts learn—pioneering (knot tying), backpacking, canoeing, fishing, shooting, even drafting and engineering. And keep in mind this was all extracurricular.

It worked like this:

- *Select a subject you want to master.*
- *Contract with a merit badge counselor, who helps you learn.*
- *Work hard.*

- *When you are ready, your merit badge counselor tests you on the exact requirements of your subject.*
- *If you pass, your counselor signs your "blue card" and orders your merit badge.*

One of Budd's many merit badges was for camping. Sure, camping was fun. It was also rigorous. Budd completed most requirements for his Boy Scout camping merit badge at Camp Everglades—a natural, 253 acre campground within Everglades National Park.

Boy Scouts of America
Camping Merit Badge Requirements

Camping is one of the best-known methods of the Scouting movement. When he founded the Scouting movement in the early 1900s, Robert Baden-Powell encouraged every Scout to learn the art of living out-of-doors. He believed a young person able to take care of himself while camping would have the confidence to meet life's other challenges, too.

Requirements

Do the following:

Explain to your counselor the most likely hazards you may encounter while participating in camping activities and what you should do to anticipate, help prevent, mitigate, and respond to these hazards.

Show that you know first-aid for and how to prevent injuries or illnesses that could occur while camping, including hypothermia, frostbite, heat reactions, dehydration, altitude sickness, insect stings, tick bites, snakebite, blisters, and hyperventilation.

Learn the Leave No Trace principles and the Outdoor Code and explain what they mean. Write a personal and group plan for implementing these principles on your next outing.

Make a written plan for an overnight trek and show how to get to your camping spot using a topographical map and compass OR a topographical map and a GPS receiver. If no GPS receiver unit is available, explain how to use one to get to your camping spot.

Do the following:

Make a duty roster showing how your patrol is organized for an actual overnight campout. List assignments for each member.

Help a Scout patrol or a Webelos Scout unit in your area prepare for an actual campout, including creating the duty roster, menu planning, equipment needs, general planning, and setting up camp.

Do the following:

Prepare a list of clothing you would need for overnight campouts in both warm and cold weather. Explain the term "layering."

Discuss footwear for different kinds of weather and how the right footwear is important for protecting your feet.

Explain the proper care and storage of camping equipment (clothing, footwear, bedding).

List the outdoor essentials necessary for any campout, and explain why each item is needed.

Present yourself to your Scoutmaster with your pack for inspection. Be correctly clothed and equipped for an overnight campout.

Do the following:

Describe the features of four types of tents, when and where they could be used, and how to care for tents. Working with another Scout, pitch a tent.

Discuss the importance of camp sanitation and tell why water treatment is essential. Then demonstrate two ways to treat water.

Describe the factors to be considered in deciding where to pitch your tent.

Tell the difference between internal- and external-frame packs. Discuss the advantages and disadvantages of each.

Discuss the types of sleeping bags and what kind would be suitable for different conditions. Explain the proper care of your sleeping bag and how to keep it dry. Make a comfortable ground bed.

Prepare for an overnight campout with your patrol by doing the following:

Make a checklist of personal and patrol gear that will be needed.

Pack your own gear and your share of the patrol equipment and food for proper carrying. Show that your pack is right for quickly getting what is needed first, and that it has been assembled properly for comfort, weight, balance, size, and neatness.

Do the following:

Explain the safety procedures for:

Using a propane or butane/propane stove

Using a liquid fuel stove

Proper storage of extra fuel

Discuss the advantages and disadvantages of different types of lightweight cooking stoves.

Prepare a camp menu. Explain how the menu would differ from a menu for a backpacking or float trip. Give recipes and make a food list for your patrol. Plan two breakfasts, three lunches, and two suppers.

Discuss how to protect your food against bad weather, animals, and contamination.

Cook at least one breakfast, one lunch, and one dinner for your patrol from the meals you have planned for requirement 8c. At least one of those meals must be a trail meal requiring the use of a lightweight stove.

Show experience in camping by doing the following:

Camp a total of at least 20 nights at designated Scouting activities or events.* One long-term camping experience of up to six consecutive nights may be applied toward this requirement. Sleep each night under the sky or in a tent you have pitched. If the camp provides a tent that has already been pitched, you need not pitch your own tent.

On any of these camping experiences, you must do TWO of the following, only with proper preparation and under qualified supervision.

Hike up a mountain, gaining at least 1,000 vertical feet.

Backpack, snowshoe, or cross-country ski for at least 4 miles.

Take a bike trip of at least 15 miles or at least four hours.

Take a non-motorized trip on the water of at least four hours or 5 miles.

Plan and carry out an overnight snow camping experience.

Rappel down a rappel route of 30 feet or more.

Perform a conservation project approved by the landowner or land managing agency.

Discuss how the things you did to earn this badge have taught you about personal health and safety, survival, public health, conservation, and good citizenship. In your discussion, tell how Scout spirit and the Scout Oath and Scout Law apply to camping and outdoor ethics.

Windley Key

Budd wrote in his diary . . .

Getting ready for camp . . .

    ✓ Wax everything first thing
    ✓ Make simple writing table
    ✓ Fix all screens
    ✓ Get own targets & ammunition for private
       practice

- ✓ Fix or make a good shelf & rack for coat hangers
- ✓ Socks
- ✓ Rain-coat
- ✓ Hatchet
- ✓ Knives
- ✓ Camera—big & little
- ✓ Film
- ✓ Boots
- ✓ Dress shoes
- ✓ Moccasins
- ✓ Sneaks
- ✓ Hiking shoes
- ✓ Pr. Dungarees
- ✓ Riding britches
- ✓ 1 sheet
- ✓ 1 pillowcase
- ✓ pr. mismatched pajamas
- ✓ white towels
- ✓ 1 pr. white tennis shorts
- ✓ 1 green dress shirt
- ✓ 6 pr. sweat socks
- ✓ 2 polo shirts
- ✓ 2 pr. undershorts
- ✓ 5 handkerchiefs

Doesn't seem like Sunday at all. Got up at five. Got to camp at approx. 1:00 P.M. All I had was several slices of bread and some raisins. Rushed and left Hyall & Dodson about 2:00 P.M. and we hiked onto the shelter at Ross's Knob. Got there about 2 hours before they had. Hard grade. Had meat for a change—corn, bread, soup, & beans and cocoa. Crossed Hell Ridge in the aft. & it was

HOT, ROCKY & no water. Was overwhelmed by the majesty of the scenery.

Was up at 6:45 A.M. Started out at bottom of White Rock. Went about two hours to get to Daven Point Gap. Had 5 solid miles of downhill grade. Saw bear signs again all along where they had been eating soft wood—signs on every bark tree. Went down to Mt. Sterling stood in CC truck and met car there. While there I went swimming in hole in big creek.

Came back at 8 P.M. Mr. Hudson is a dope at times—tried to put a halter on from the front. Dumb Bell!!! Rode and beat Mooney twice with halter. Rode Grey bareback & she threw me. Boy am I sore!!

Up & Exercise. Took out second group. Rode Tammy. Signed up for competition today—tennis, swimming, & rifle. Had lunch with Bob today. Show tonite. Very, very busy, but will continue reading my books and, of course, my Bible!!!

Went hiking. Then came back and went swimming. Dove off a high tree at swimming place—about 20 feet. Highest of life so far. Joe and I sneaked to store and spent a quarter. Came back had supper. Apple pie for dessert then roasted marshmallows. Played football after supper.

Bed & THEN . . .

Good Morning—What a day at camp!!! This morning at 8:05 AM PV and I were rudely awakened by an over powering stench. Applejack

Molby didn't have enough will power to contain the 2 Carter's Little Liver Pills we slipped him in a piece of candy. BOY! I thought we'd die laughing. He got over to the dresser & whined that he couldn't find any pajamas & all the while shooting a stream. That went on until he left another "patch" in the hall.

Rained all morning. Cleaned up room!!! We senior counselors met to work on the best all around camper grades. After lunch a bunch of us got Bebo down and shaved his chest. Boy was he sad!!!

Then shot the rifle & bow and arrow. Won 10 candy bars. Had a short swim (COOOLLLLDDD!) Saddled horses and rode 'til it started to rain again. Cleaned out barn. Watered, curried, & fed horses. Messed around & then after supper went and saw "Horse Opera." Read the Army book on horsemanship and Bible.

Good Nite!!!

Budd's love of camping didn't end with Boy Scouts.

Christmas dinner at Windley Key, 1949

On July 19, 1943, Budd wrote in his diary . . .

> PV and I were loaded and on the road by 9:00. By 10:00 we were at the ice house loading ice. The trip up the canal was fine. Saw a small gator, snakes, gar (!), turtles, birds, and what have you. PV gigged several gar as we went by. Went over dam about 3:00. We began looking for a campsite. There wasn't a hammock in 25 miles! Finally I spotted a low spot in the mound along the bank and we made it do. Leveled it off, pulled weeds, and generally cleaned it up. Mosquitoes? MILLIONS literally!!! Pitched tent and had a fire going when the rains came.

> After it was over we built another fire and finally ate about dark. Then to bed—for almost 40 whole minutes; at 10:10 I said, "Are you asleep?" . . . "Yes!" "Well let's get the damn hell outa' here." We left and at 3:45 we were at the back door

talking to Dad. It was a nice trip back, cold at times, and cramped! Was quite a job loading and unloading in the dark. But that's camping!!

The Boy Scouts of America was founded in 1910. Boy Scouts advance through ranks—Scout, Tenderfoot, Second class, First class, Star, Life. And, ultimately, Eagle. By 2012, slightly over 80 million boys passed through various ranks. But only slightly over two million—*2 percent*—earned their Eagle feather.

Budd Post was one.

Eagle Scouts:

- ✓ Earn at least 21 merit badges
- ✓ Deomonstrate Scout Spirit through the Boy Scout Oath and Law
- ✓ Demonstrate leadership in the troop, team, crew, or ship
- ✓ Plan, develop, lead, and manage a service project—the Eagle Project—that benefits his school, religious institution, or community
- ✓ Participate in a Scoutmaster conference
- ✓ Complete an Eagle Scout board of review

Proud Eagle Scout

On October 13, 1938, Budd Post sat alongside his parents. The scoutmaster from Troop 1, Miami Florida stood. He unfolded his script. He spoke . . .

"Howard M. Post—Budd—please come forward with your parents.

You see that I hold here a feather. This is not just any feather, but represents that of an eagle, the most respected of all creatures. The eagle is most beloved by the Great Spirit because it represents life and how all things are divided into two parts.

The eagle, you see, has only two eggs at a time. Likewise, there is man and woman. People have two hands, two feet, and two eyes. We each have a body and a soul. There is also day and night, light and dark, summer and winter, war and peace, life and death.

We smell good scents and foul odors, and we see beautiful and distasteful sights. We hear pleasant sounds and dreadful news. We use our hands for good deeds, or bad.

We have before us two paths. Scouting encourages us to follow the way of good, of bravery, service, honor, and brotherhood. We also may choose selfishness, laziness, mean spirit, and deceit. That choice belongs to each of us.

On your journey, you have chosen the Scouting way, and through your work you have earned the Eagle rank. Wear the patch you receive proudly. I also present to each of you a feather of your own. When you see it, remember what it represents, that we face choices every day which path we will follow. Stay true, and continue on your trail of the Eagle."

The scoutmaster pinned the mother's oval pin, the father's oval pin, the mentor's oval pin, the Eagle badge, and the Eagle award medal to the left shirt pocket of Budd's Scout uniform. He handed Budd his Eagle feather.

Jean cried.

Harry puffed up.

And Budd? Well, Budd just grinned his unassuming grin.

Yet, in his heart he knew . . . *Once an Eagle, always an Eagle.*

Eagles are prepared. For life.

7.

You're in the Army Now—Except

Like father, like son. The Christian Bible safeguards these timeless words.

In John 5:19-23, Jesus says,

"I tell you the solemn truth, the Son can do nothing on his own initiative, but only what He sees the Father doing. For whatever the Father does, the Son does likewise. For the Father loves the Son and shows Him everything He does, and greater deeds than these He will show Him, so that you may be amazed. For just as the Father raises the dead and gives them life, so also the Son gives life to whomever He wishes. Furthermore, the Father does not judge anyone, but has assigned all judgment to the Son, so that all people may honor the Son just as they honor the Father. The one who does not honor the Son does not honor the Father who sent him."

Some theologians suggest Jesus's words are the most meaningful text in the Gospel of John—actually, the most meaningful text in the entire New Testament. Others argue they are the very foundation of the entire Christian faith.

Perhaps Budd considered Jesus's lesson when he followed his father's footsteps and became a military man. Perhaps he did not. We do not know for certain.

We do know that 15-year-old Budd Post wrote in his diary . . .

> Was looking over Dad's war souvenirs & <u>GOD,</u> what feelings they bring.

We do know the Post military tradition goes back to World War I, when Harry Post served in the United States Army. The First World War—*The Great War*—was a global war, centered in Europe. The conflict started on June 28, 1914, with the assassination of Austria's Archduke Franz Ferdinand and his wife Sophie.

Between 1914 and 1917, the Allied Forces (France, United Kingdom, Russia) and the Central Powers (Germany, Austria-Hungary) fired artillery and lobbed grenades from trenches. They raced across "no man's land" on foot, only to be felled by machine gun fire and artillery. Millions of young men were slaughtered. It was a war of attrition—the side with the most men left standing would win.

The Allies needed help. They hoped the United States would garner its vast resources and fight on their side. But the United States clung to isolationism—why should it get involved in a war so far away—a war without any direct effect on America or Americans?

Well, on May 7, 1915, a German U-boat sank the British ocean liner RMS *Lusitania*. The *Lusitania* was neutral—a luxury ship commissioned for pleasure, not war. Still, of the 1,959 civilian passengers onboard, 1,198 drowned. Over 100 hundred were U.S. citizens. Americans were shocked. Outraged. Tension between the United States and Germany erupted. Slowly, Americans began to rethink their standoffish position.

Then, in January 1917, Germany's Foreign Minister, Arthur Zimmerman, sent a coded telegram to Germany's Mexican Ambassador, Heinrich von Eckhard. British intelligence agents intercepted. The deciphered message revealed Germany's plan for unrestricted submarine warfare and offered U.S. territory to Mexico, if Mexico would declare war on the United States. Overnight, the war machine advanced toward America's borders.

On April 6, 1917, newspaper headlines around the world shouted the news: **U.S. PRESIDENT WOODROW WILSON SIGNS WAR DECREE! CALLS VOLUNTEERS!** "Over there" beckoned. Americans responded.

The fighting continued for another year. Millions more died. Then, in 1918, on the 11th hour, of the 11th day, of the 11th month, the fighting ended. Germany signed the armistice at Compiegne, France. Bells tolled. *The Great War* was officially over.

Excerpts from letters written by 24-four-year-old Harry E. Post (#1360037), from Ordnance Depot, Hqrs., 1ˢᵗ Depot Div., Am. E.F. A.P.O.727, St. Aignan, France, provide perspective . . .

Harry E. Post, Ready to Ride, U.S. Cavalry

England
July 2-18
Dear Grandma—

Have arrived safely on land—Didn't even see a "sub."
We are preparing to go by rail to a camp now. Will write
you a letter as soon as I get in camp.

Lots of love,
Harry

****

At Sea
June 1918
Dear Folks:

Still traveling the Deep Blue. Have made the trip so
far like a boy on the way to a circus. The seas have been
splendid and pretty most of the way. One day we ran into
a storm which treated us rather roughly. The ship however
acted pretty much the girl she is with the exception of
pulling off some rough stunts—such as riding the waves
with her hands in the air and diving too deep when she
didn't notify us.

I kept the fish guessing though for about 3 hours—
and I managed to fool them. I don't think I'll get sea-
sick on this trip, and right now I feel "Bully" or as the
Englishmen will have it—"Bloody Fine." The lemons
Aunt Florence gave me, I'm sorry to say, went to the bad

before I had an occasion to use them. The other stuff came in handy. This is all I know at present. Will surely write you upon arrival on land. It'll feel good to plant a foot on solid ground again.

Lots of love to all,
Harry

P.S.—Write soon. Don't put France or England on envelope—I might be in the Philippines for all you know or I either.

****

July 7, 1918
France
Dear Folks:

Still too far away to be in hearing distance of activities going on in the war zone.—We however, are beginning to realize more and more each day that we are really at war, and not just merely in the army. Not just because we are hearing the zone of man-slaughter, but because we feel it in our immediate surroundings. At present, I'm at another "rest camp." At least that's what it is called. You can use your own judgment as to what I think about it.—But taking all into consideration, before this thing is over, I guess I would be glad if I could just only get back here for a rest.

Our travel route through England couldn't have been better. The country was magnificent—most beautiful have ever seen and I have been in a number of good old USA states. The part we have seen in France thus far has also been wonderful—probably all of this is due to the fact that every square inch of ground is being unitized for some purpose. You have read and heard in the papers of how England had to do in regards to food rations and about the girls and women working. I did too, when I was in the states and imagined lots of things.—But, you really can't begin to realize what a fix England is in. Just imagine—one family regardless of size can't buy, beg, or steal more than 2 ozs. of butter per week and one pound of meat a week.—and everything else is practically the same condition—and as for sugar—you would think England didn't know such a product ever existed.

The railroads of England are certainly a curiosity.— Their engines aren't much bigger than our "toy" engines and the coaches resemble a "cab" and box cars resemble a big hay wagon. The cars have only 4 wheel all told—and the wheels have spokes like a wheelbarrow. But, I must admit they can make several miles per hour.

We probably will move from here to a training camp in a day or so. After we have our stay in training camp we will then gradually begin our move up to the front line and the sooner I can get into the fray the better I will like it. "Excitement" is my name from now on—I love it—and as for my nervous system it's just the finest kind, so I'm not worrying one bit of the outcome.

I was mighty glad I had the opportunity to see you when I was at Camp Merritt. It did me worlds of good—more than you can imagine—and I promise it will never be another 3 years that I stay away from home—that is if I get back to the states before that and I believe we will if Uncle Sam puts 4 million men over here by January as he says he will. Time is getting short as well as this paper is running low—will write again when I have the opportunity.

Love to all,
Harry

****

Over Here
July 12, 1918
Dear Grandma:

    Still safe and sound. Am too far from the front line to hear the "Big Guns" but I can feel war more than ever before—mostly by my <u>luxurious accommodations</u>—taking it all in tho', it is much better than I expected and after all why complain—It could be lots worse—As for choice of armies—there never was but <u>One Uncle Sam</u>.
    I am located at a French town called St. Aignan. What part of France it is in I don't know. I have traveled around so much I don't know which direction I have gone in. I guess these houses around here must have been built 500 years ago. They look t anyway—and further, you can't find a nail in the structure. The beams are all wedged in order to hold its places.
    I am feeling fine—and now going to school (ordnance school). This school will last for a period of about 30

days—so you see, I will probably be settled here for that length of time.—But I don't look to stay in one place as long as that again.

Everything here is on the move all the time—so I never know what to expect. The sooner I go up to the front the better I will like it—I want to get into the excitement—I know hardships will be attached—But I can stand them if anybody can.

With reference to American soldiers—Over in the states everywhere you go you see Uncle Sam's Boys. Over here it is identically the same—you see the American uniform everywhere. Of course you see the other Allied uniforms—none like the U.S. tho.

America will never be beaten—it's just a small matter of time now before the war will be over—Just get the men over here and see—The morale of the U.S. Boys is a wonderful thing compared to others. The boys have no fear at all. We'll do just as the YMCA man said—"We will fight them' till hell freezes over and then buy skates and go after them on sea."

Still looking for mail.

Lovingly,
Harry

****

Somewhere in France
Sunday—July 28, 1918
Dear Grandma and Folks:

This has been surely a lonesome day, but I guess it could have been a lot worse. Sometimes, I wish I could be right "up there" in the excitement—But some of us (which is a large number too) have to stay behind and look out for those "up there"—and I happen to be one of the fortunate so far.

The Ordnance Department is a non-combatant organization, so for the present, I might consider myself safe—Not that I'm afraid to go up to the lines.—Definitely no!!—and before it is over I hope to have had my crack at the dirty "hun"—But, it's like this—none of us want to die—I don't meant that it means death to go up—because it doesn't—There's 90% chances of coming back or recovering from a wound—But someone has to do that "backing up" for the fellows that are up there, so, you see I'm fortunate in that way—If need be—I'll stand right where others have fallen—What's death when it's covered with glory?

And yet, if you are doing your part as I am, why take the chances?—The government needs me here as bad as on the lines, perhaps more—So, I'll stay and stick for a promotion. The Ordnance Department is the highest branch of Army service.

Just heard some good news about the war—This "Allied Drive" makes things look good, doesn't it?

That's about all I know now—All I am wanting now is a letter from you.

Love and best wishes to all,
Harry

****

August 16, 1918
Dear Folks:

Several days have elapsed since I last wrote. Still a "Buck private" and it now looks as though my status will remain as it is for duration of war—It's hard in one way after being a Sergeant for almost two years, a recommendation for commission, a candidate at Officers Training School, only to be thrown out for cause of operation. Oh Well! It could be far worse if I were out in ranks.

The army has a lot of poor men in good places and vise-versa. Office work is usually routine, throughout, and it doesn't make a world of difference if you have a title or not. My official job title is "accountant." So taking it "all in all" why feel discouraged? However, if I had been fortunate enough to remain with Captain Lubeek of the Ordnance Dept (You remember him at Camp Merritt) I feel sure I would have been promoted—old hard luck jumped in tho' and spoiled it. Captain Lubeek however did me a good turn by writing on my Service Record "Recommended for Ordnance Sergeant." Whether that recommendation will eventually mean anything, is to be found out.

As the old saying goes—this leaves me well and happy—and truly does. I hope this letter will find you in the same spirits.

Lots of love
Harry

****

Sunday Sept 1st
Hello Everybody:

Received your letter of August 8th today. Your letters are precious.

Ice cream! Good gracious what is that? Oh yes, I remember the last time I saw that was in Camp Merritt— and American candy—No!!—Things of that nature don't inhabit this place. "Ice" is a luxury and is to be found only in the larger cities of France. I haven't had a good cold drink of that nature since leaving the states.

I want to go out on replacement to some Division on the Front. Have spoken to the captain about it, but as yet I have received no decision. My motive for this is first, I want to get near the actual war game—Secondly a man could stick here for months and months and never get a promotion. Not that I feel that I'm due one—But because good men worthy of promotions have been here a long time and under present conditions are liable to be here a good while longer. Waiting for a promotion here would be like an angel coming to me with a plate full of ice cream.

We have been eating "corn willies" for the past 10 days and may have to do so for 10 more. Fresh beef doesn't seem to be available—maybe a "sub" got to one of our cargo ships—Can't kick, getting good food under the circumstances.

The government has a "Sales Commissary" here—which supplies our demands for cigarettes, jam, and toilet articles at a very reasonable price—Yes, we do get some candy too—stick put up in cans. The YMCA has chocolate and a very few sweet cakes for sale for about 14 cents. With my $34.30 per month net pay I have plenty of money to buy what I want.

Don't forget to put the A.P.O. address on your letters—will get here faster.

Love to all,
Harry

****

November 12, 1918
Dear Folks:

The war is over!! Enough said.
Be home soon!

Love
Harry

****

France
Jan. 17-1919
Dear Folks:

Still awaiting orders to proceed towards a base port. So you see, even though a schedule calls for a certain date—often times it doesn't mean that the movement will be put in execution at that specific time. We are expecting to start any day—yet we may be here until the 1st of February.

Now just what I'll do when I get out of the service all depends upon the arrangements I can make with the manager of the Southern Executive office at Atlanta. Wherever I am mustered out transportation will be furnished to me by Uncle Sam to the place I enlisted which is Atlanta.

I stand well with the Woolworth Company and don't see any reason (after seeing mgr.) why I couldn't relocate in the NY office. And too—I am personally acquainted with the chief auditor of the Woolworth Co. whose headquarters is in the NY office.

I am going to put all my effort into getting placed as an assistant manager in one of the Woolworth stores. I'm not sure if I am "ripe" for that just yet. If not, I will probably locate in the NY office. Should I succeed in this though—I will have to go wherever placed—and too, if I should be so fortunate my assignment would come from the Southern office—and in all probability to some southern city under supervision of the office. However, at present that's neither here nor there—I'll have to wait until I get out of the Army to see what developments can be made.

I am mighty glad Howard will share his "bed"—and am mighty anxious to be back with you again even if I have to build a "bunk" in the cellar I should be glad. Sorry to hear that you are ill again Grandma—But I hope that by the time this reaches you—you will be feeling in 1st class shape. Glad to know Howard had only a light touch of the "flu" because it seems to be a pretty dangerous thing to fool with.

Each time I write I keep saying "This is my last letter from France"—But, so long as we are delayed and the opportunity presents itself, I will be letting you know how things are going.

Love to all,
Harry

****

France

Jan. 23—1919

Dear Folks:

The latest "dope" now is that we will leave here Sunday the 26th—From all indications it looks as though we will get away this time—we probably won't be on the high seas until Feb. 10 or 11.

81

Will let you know as soon as I land what becomes of me—a proud military man. And now in the meantime if our orders are not changed—this will be my last letter from France.

Lots of Love
Au Revoir
Harry

Like his father before him, Budd followed family tradition and became "a proud military man." It all started at Marion Military Institute, in Marion, Alabama.

Founded in 1842, by Colonel James Thomas Murfee, Marion Military Institute is the oldest military junior college in America. It stands on tradition: Truth. Honor. Service. Its mission is to "educate and train the Corps of Cadets in order that each graduate is prepared for success at four-year institutions, including the service academies." Its reputation is preeminent. Unique. Legendary.

And as 18-year-old Budd Post soon discovered, Marion's commitment to honor, intellectual challenges, moral and ethical expectations, physical and athletic prowess, and innovative leadership is demanding. Or in the vernacular, "a downright killer."

Between July 14, 1942, when Budd entered Marion, and May 25, 1943, when he graduated, he recorded his experiences, accomplishments, and occasional woes in his diary . . .

Good Morning—left Tallahassee about 8:15. Had lunch at Selma, Ala. We got to Marion about 2:15. The town is nothing—the school would take all night to describe. Suffice to say—I'll be here & will study like hell to make the apt. Mom and Dad had supper here then said good bye and here I am. Can't go to sleep till 11:30. Oh me!!!

I miss most of all, having close friends about—its largely impersonal here—considering it, though, I kinda like it.

Routine is the same—up 7:20, make bed, dress, calisthenics, drill, inspection, breakfast formation, 5 hours of classes, lunch, chapel, some activity (swim, basketball, softball, etc.) more drill, piddle around (some), supper, 2-3 hours of solid study, write letters, study through late lites, read Bible, then, shut-eye, and Good Nite! It's a downright killer!!!

Durn it's awful hard. Had to see a Map Reading movie at 5:00. Saw the West point Yearbook for '42 in library. I'm just as well satisfied to go in '44—boy, I bet the studies are really tough!!!

Am reading "King Lear", again. Got into a crap game just before supper and lost six bits—I don't know what's the matter with me.

Exam Day!!! The Great Day!!! Here's hopin! The first exam started at 9:30 in the library. The type of examination had been changed from what we had studied. Was pretty rough—did about 86 I would guess. It took 7 ½ hours for the 4 subjects and I worked the limit on every one.

After supper we cleaned up and went to Judson. "A" Co. moved out about 8:30. I didn't get a date, but did see a couple who I am going to meet.

The mornings grow cooler and steadily darker. Colonel Baer spoke on obedience, command, reason, and duty. Gosh, I must not fall behind. I started drawing after supper and forgot to stop until 3:15 in the morning.

Was "on hall" tonight for first time. Damnation!!! You see, after taps we raised holy ____; fighting, dumping mattresses over, throwing shoes, books, etc. We also busted a lamp. This morning we heard about it. "Disturbance . . ." I have too much free time. That will change—I was elected leader of my discussion club—probably because we had a diagnostic test in English, and I made the highest grade in school. Club has great possibilities. We got off onto religion by accident and that is the topic for the next time. We have a good Orthodox Jew among us, Catholics, Baptists, Methodists, Presbyterians, Episcopalians, etc.

Have just returned from seeing "Mrs. Miniver"— may there be more pictures as powerful as that. It made quite an impression upon me—all about courage amid chaos and loss. I hope I recover in time to study this week! Followed usual schedule today, but did not run (except back from the movies as was sure I was late!) Received letters from PV and Suzanne today—must read them again, the show drove them out of my mind.

From now on I shall try to record more of my feelings in this diary—to make it more worthwhile. However, my own style will undoubtedly seem interesting enough in 50 years!!!

After supper we marched to Judson and heard "The Master Singers"—a male quartet—very, very good. The battalion behaved like a bunch of kids; they hooted and hollered, gave "15" for Errol Flynn, Dickey Bird, and generally acted boorishly. After it was over we marched back, and I drew for a little while. Must study valiance.

Tried to sleep, but finally wound up at the P.C. gym. We practiced a while and then supper. After supper went to a meeting of the captains of the platoon soft ball teams (me being Capt., second platoon, A Co)

After supper signed out to town & a date. She failed to show up and I saw "Andy Hardy's Double Life" alone. I now know she called this afternoon to tell me she "couldn't" but that knocker Heming said he was too lazy to hunt me up, and I never got the call. I ought to knock his block off!

I wonder if Hitler is really responsible for the war or is it human nature? Do we never learn?

Bought another watermelon this aft. with Stone. Ate it, and incidentally, spent 50¢ in church, and an even dollar on shaving cream and brush, which leaves me flat broke. Also—lost two dollars in a crap game—and I was a dollar ahead a couple times. Am glad my money is gone. Now I'll quit wasting it!!!

Had first tactical problem—as buck-ass private I did nothing but lay on my face on a hill crest & fight ants. Was hot and rugged.

Continue to read Bible—mine & Plebes' Bible from West Point. Very educational.

Classes were punk today. Went down to Dick's after supper for a bottle of milk. Should have studied, but wrote 10 letters to Admiral Kesner, Dad, Mom, Aunt Flossie, PV. Isy, Stubb, etc.—Susy can wait for all I care!!! Received an important letter from Dad today—tuition check ($384) and my allowance.

Called Mom and Dad. Dad wants to know if I want to go to Miami U. and get in the reserves. It's definite that I'll stay here this year. Boy, did I have the red ass for a while. After supper, my name was read out to appear in the math building at 6:30—yes, I was selected for the Cotillion Club. Hot dog!

Colonel Bair gave a 20 minute talk on the motto of the school (truth, honor, & service) Bought a second hand uniform for $17.50—will save me about $20.00. Oh boy!

Up at 5:30 to study. Did fair on my exam—97%. My algebra grade will be 75-80. NUTS. Finished "Forsyth Saga" after supper and it was well worth reading.

Didn't feel good—tried to sleep during CQ and Dickey Bird was OC—he came around 5 times trying to catch me. May get stuck for that one.

After supper had a lecture on light by a man who worked with Edison—smart & extremely interesting. Studied after the lecture until release when I took time out to put some stuff on my jock itch. It has literally & absolutely blistered some of my skin; it's still burning after 1½ hours!!!

After supper is when fun started—this is last week as underclassman—we will really catch it this week. We had to sing a lot and then double-time a while.

After supper went to a lecture on current affairs by Captain Schiller (I ate my whole supper with a knife—including ice cream).

Did fair on lit composition—75%, but it was third highest grade in class. This shit's hard!! Did punk in history—only 90 for month. Then, I flunked the dog shit out of math. I am truly ashamed of myself—ashamed that I disappointed Mom and Dad.

After supper went to town and saw "Sweater Girl"—a college murder mystery, and very interesting "B" picture it was, especially for 15¢.

Then back to school and danced till midnight—Judson girls were there—didn't get along satisfactorily at all—their dancing is punk and knowledge of formalities about the same. Boy was I tired!

Listened to the radio after supper. For posterity, the top tunes of the 1942 Hit Parade were "My Devotion," "Be Careful, It's My Heart," and "I Got a Gal in Kalamazoo."

Dress parade in clean fatigues today. I carried the flag again. After supper worked on Mech Drawing and learned the rudiments of the machine gun—disassembling, etc.—managed to earn a 90 in mechanical drawing for the month, and he said my drawings were OK—my shrouded pulley was a flop, but not from the drawing angle; it was mechanically faulty. Oh well, I'm learning.

About 5 minutes before CQ, the man on the hall called everybody together and said Mazarra was going to stick everyone because someone had told Major Addis that he was not inspecting right. It seems that my complainings yesterday were responsible. This morning everybody, including myself, got stuck for 3. Everybody was sore at me, and I confess that I did pull a boner. Me, who has lived for good-conduct list!!! Technically I am open to false O.S. charges. Oh well, I like to walk. Note to self: Horse sense is something a horse has that keeps him from betting on people!!!

After supper saw some lantern slides for first year military. My military science and training class is getting right interesting. Had test in MS & T—did terrible but Sargent Magarra is a punk teacher. I AM a military man!! I'll be the best before it's over!!! After supper read West Point Book of Knowledge.

Had formation this morning and then completed written tests on drill and command, rifle, marksmanship, military sanitation & first aid, tactical training, and organization of infantry—sure I did well even though I have a terrific case of Red Ass.

About midnight we heard a riot in South. Major Lewis went over & durned if they hadn't put the school mule in his room!!

This morning heard speakers from all 5 armed services urging us to join. I am ARMY, like my dad. After supper received the news: I ranked 16th in the prospective drill platoon candidate competition. Hot dog!! Went to town on a Dean's list leave. All the "sakes" are back—the dopes—all the drinking they do—NUTS!!!

Up at 6:15 to shine buttons. We paraded uptown and massed in the square; taps was played in a duet. It was beautiful. After supper we had a tactical problem. I was the runner. I enjoyed it. Then ran around the block & did pushups before studying. (Grades came out—made Dean's List again.) We are using the Manual of Arms.

Saw Captain Wilson and had him analyze my reading ability—it can be improved (what

can't???) but not bad. Had road march today—
feeling great—Smith praised my battalion for
our cleanup & then saluted an unbelievable,
"Dismissed!!" After supper read the Miami
Herald and learned the Allies are doing okay
apparently—hope it keeps me out of the draft a
while longer. But must register at the draft board.
The year is fast running out (1942). I hope my
diary is a good account of my year. The year 1943
should prove extremely eventful. I pray that Mom
& Dad will have a happy successful year & that
the war will end this year. (I dreamed last night
that it would—possibly it may be, but just for
me!) "May the Lord bless you & keep you & give
you holy peace. Amen." Went to church 33 times
this year. An improvement!!

Had chemistry quiz and I didn't know shit
from shoe polish. Oh well. I'll make it. Went to
show with Virginia Mitchell—Western—self-
explanatory! Coming back I met a big possum
in the road—he came within 2 feet of me before
he realized it. Called Mom and Dad—was finally
connected about 17:40. Explained my current
draft deferment to them, and told them about
my order to report for induction to the Army on
July 6, 1943.

Yes. Uncle Sam wanted Howard Malvern Post. Order
No. 12231, signed by Brigadier General Vivian Collins,
Florida State Director of Selective Service was official.
Very official. Budd's orders read, "Howard Malvern Post is

to report, at 6:30 AM, on the 6th day of July, 1943, to City Hall, Hialeah, Dade, Fla."

Budd, along with millions of other draft-eligible men, were told, "It is imperative that each man do his part. Every one of us has a task to perform. Yours is the part of a soldier—a service upon which tradition imposes a high honor. Upon your shoulders rests the faith of your neighbors, whose chosen representative you are."

The induction notice acknowledged that life would be different. New. But if draftees followed suggestions, "the road through it would be smoother . . .

Go to it cheerfully, soberly, and alertly. On your journey from your local board to the Induction Station, obey the instructions of your leader. Be mindful of the property of the public carriers as any damage to same will be your responsibility.

Also remember you are entering this new life with the eyes of your associates watching your every action. Therefore, your conduct in the beginning may have a lasting influence on the success that you hope to attain in this business of being a good soldier.

Travel light. If you wish, take a small bag with a few clean clothes, a few handkerchiefs, socks, soap, towel, and necessary toilet articles. These are not essential as you will be issued necessary equipment by the army, but they may come in handy should there be any delay in your induction into the service.

Leave jewelry, large sums of money, and other valuables at home, for they may easily be lost. If possible take a little spending money for such needs as you may have before your first pay-day. Take some postal cards or stationery and stamps, a fountain pen, and an inexpensive watch if you have them.

Leave your automobile or motorcycle at home.

It takes time for the army to assign you to your permanent military unit. Keep in touch with your friends and family, but ask them not to write to you until you have a definite and complete address to which mail will be delivered. As soon as you are inducted into the army your nearest relatives will be advised as to your whereabouts, so don't worry about being out of touch with your family in the event of an emergency.

At the Reception Center, the army will classify you, that is, try to find the type of job in the army which you can do best, in which you will be happiest and do the best for yourself and for your country. Before you go to the classifier, think back over all the jobs you have had, how long you worked at them, and EXACTLY WHAT YOU YOURSELF DID IN THEM. Give all the information honestly and completely. It will be for your best interest.

Go to the army with an open mind and forget any ideas which you now have unless you KNOW they are correct. Keep your ears and eyes open. Obey others in the best way you know how and you will succeed.

Your country needs your help, otherwise you would not have been called. Some of us will not have the privilege of serving as you serve. Our work will be in other fields—fields of related endeavor. With your assistance all of us will achieve our common goal—the maintenance of the free heritage to which we were born.

VIVIAN COLLINS
BRIGADIER GENERAL AGD
STATE DIRECTOR
OF
SELECTIVE SERVICE

Form
Fla SS 11
3-11-42

In addition, per Form, Fla. SS5, inductees were granted the privilege of applying for life insurance, as provided in the National Service Life Insurance Act of 1940, in any amounts from $1,000 to $10,000, in multiples of $500. Monthly premiums, for each $1,000, ranged from 64¢, for 18-year-olds, to 95¢, for 44-year-olds.

That very evening, Harry typed a letter to Local Draft Board #2, in Hialeah, Florida:

871 Lake Drive,
Miami Springs, Fla.

April 2, 1943.

Local Board #2
Dade County,
Hialeah, Fla.

Dear Sirs:

Howard Malvern Post, my son, presumably will soon be eligible for call to service. If, under the regulations a postponement can be granted, may I respectfully urge your consideration for a short delay in the issuance of the call for the following reasons:

#1. His college year and present semester ending, at the Marion Military Institute, Marion, Ala. will be terminated May 24th.

#2. Postponement of induction call will permit him the opportunity of earning and establishing the credits for a completed years' work.

#3. After his service with Uncle Sam, these credits will provide the qualifications necessary to college re-entry and the continuance of his education without which he will lose the time, effort, progress and investment already made.

Hoping this request will receive your considered attention and that favorable action can be taken, I remain,

Respectfully yours,

——————————

(H. E. Post)

Harry's request was granted. Budd continued at Marion until May 25, 1943.

Budd wrote in his dairy . . .

> Today I sat all alone and just thought. I thought about: How I loved Mom and Dad; how glad I'd be to get home; how I would hate the Japs if they killed prisoners as rumored; the work that remains this semester. And then a random thought—I just happened to recall the putt I made for a birdie on #18 at the Biltmore to beat Whiffy Cox for the handicap championship. I went to bed with a generally punk feeling. Wonder what will happen to me?
>
> Had Sponsor's Day parade. Everybody had a fine time. The platoon formed at 2:15 and we practiced until 3:15 when the battalion marched to Judson. On the way back we showed some spirit. We also hit upon a yell spontaneously—1-2-3-4—We're the best; there ain't no rest—1-2-3-4! The BEST. That's ME.

Well, getting ready to leave. For the first time in my life I am "on my own" more or less. What's next?

What a day! After breakfast went to Judson for Baccalaureate sermon. I sang with the choir. After serving supper I stopped in and batted the breeze with Toffle, etc. Finally called a cab and went to Judson—had a wonderful time.

Graduation Day. I ushered. During the address Pedro Acosta (Puerto Rico) broke down and left chapel. He cried to beat the cars because the boys were leaving. "You Americans are such damn fine fellows!"—a real compliment! Was surprised when I was presented with the best private medal.

Finished packing. After breakfast a few goodbyes and then to B'ham with Major Lewis. Had dinner and haircut. Then saw "Crash Drive"—only fair. After supper went to "Pride of the Yankees"—very good and a fine tribute to Lou Gehrig. Caught train at 10:07 with no time to spare but going home for at least the summer!!!

⸻

During the summer of 1943, Budd dated, danced, and stole kisses. He had his heart broken. Then, he got his teeth fixed (gold inlays). He wrote letters, read the Bible, and went to church. He saw movies at the Olympia. (Sometimes he and his date even sat in the "Colored Section.") He fed pigeons in Bayfront Park. He went out to supper with Mom and Dad and ate hamburgers at Bill's with PV. He and PV shot frogs in the Glades, ate frog legs, swam, and waded out to Marathon Island. Then, he suffered from sunburn. He played cards with Aunt Mary and Uncle Charlie. He bought roses for Mom on Mother's Day and a box of Tampa Nuggets for Dad on Father's Day. He played tennis and ping pong. He drank Coca-colas. He bought black market gasoline and drove to Naples. Then, he got a traffic ticket for parking on the beach. He messed around. And Budd played golf—lots of golf.

Budd wrote in his diary . . .

> Good Morning: Played 36 holes today, again, and have yet to play a good nine—41-44-44-41. PUNK! Dam it. On way home from church bought an "extra" and learned that Mussolini had been ousted. It's funny how I can be concerned with a golf game at the same time such a history making event is taking place. I hope to be part of World War II soon. Every young man worth his salt wants a crack at German and Jap hides!!!

07 DEC 1941

0700 hours, Hawaiian time

Two U.S. Army privates snapped to full alert. They stared at their radar screens. What the . . . Were more than fifty unidentified planes *really* approaching from the northeast?

They called their superior officer. "Don't worry, boys. The anomaly is probably part of an unexpected delivery of new B-17s coming from mainland United States," he said.

The "intel" was wrong.

The radar blip was the first wave of Japanese planes that struck the United States Naval Base at Pearl Harbor, Hawaii Territory. Commander Mitsuo Fuchida, leader of the attack, shouted, "Tora! Tora! Tora!" ("Tiger! Tiger! Tiger!")—a coded message informing the Japanese Navy that Americans were caught by surprise.

At 0758 hours, the Pearl Harbor command radioed its first message to the world: *AIR RAID, PEARL HARBOR. THIS IS NOT A DRILL.*

An hour later, a second wave of Japanese aircraft attacked. The two raids—350 planes—lasted under two hours. Still, bombs destroyed the American battleship USS *Arizona* and capsized the USS *Oklahoma*. Another 20 ships were sunk or beached. Over 310 aircraft were damaged or destroyed. Even more tragically, 2,400 Americans (military and civilian) were dead. Another 1,180 were wounded.

On December 8, at 12:30 p.m., EST, President Franklin D. Roosevelt delivered his *Day of Infamy* speech to a joint session of Congress and, via radio, the nation. The Senate responded with a unanimous vote supporting war. Only Montana pacifist, Jeanette Rankin, dissented in the House.

At 4 p.m., EST, President Roosevelt signed the declaration of war. More than two years after the conflict started in Europe, the United States of America was officially engaged in World War II—*the most deadly and destructive war in history.*

Suddenly, patriotism was popular. Americans were proud. Old Glory's red, white, and blue stirred passion in their hearts and brought tears to their eyes. "She's a grand old flag," and they would fight for her freedom. They would die for her honor.

Enthusiastic volunteers packed local draft board offices. Almost overnight, the economy shifted to war production.

By early spring 1942, mandatory gas rationing was a way of life. Gas wasn't the problem. Rubber tires were. Japanese armies had conquered the rubber-producing regions of Southeast Asia and cut off America's rubber supply. So, to conserve rubber, the government reduced the national speed limit to 35 miles an hour and issued gas ration classifications.

Gas rationing was regulated through the federal Office of Price Administration (OPA). Citizens appeared, in person, at an OPA office, certified their need for gas, and documented that they owned no more than five automobile tires (any more were confiscated). Half of all U.S. drivers were declared "nonessential" and issued black "A" windshield stickers that allowed them to buy four gallons of gas per week. For nearly a year, "A" stickered drivers were not allowed to drive for pleasure.

By March 1942, dog food was banned from metal cans. By April, civilians could not buy toothpaste unless they turned in an empty metal toothpaste tube. By May, each citizen, including babies, in the renowned *Land of Plenty* received a food ration book.

Sugar was the first consumer commodity rationed. Coffee, meat, lard, shortening, oil, cheese, eggs, jams, jellies, fruit butters, and processed foods soon followed. Women attended training sessions and learned to shop prudently, yet serve nutritious meals. Oleo margarine replaced butter. Cottage cheese substituted for meat. When shoppers discovered *two* boxes of macaroni and cheese cost *one* ration coupon, Kraft's mundane blue box became a glamorous celebrity almost overnight.

As the 1942 calendar pages turned, ration coupons were issued for liquor, cigarettes, typewriters, metal office furniture, radios, phonographs, refrigerators, vacuum cleaners, washing machines, sewing machines, stoves, fuel oil, silk, nylon, and even shoes.

Americans accepted changes the war forced on the country. While men fought in foreign battlefields, women stayed home and worked in industries that supported the war effort. After all, the government's slogan promised—*The more women at work, the sooner we win.*

More than six million Rosie the Riveters donned pants, packed lunch pails, and whistled off to do a "man's job." They built planes, bombs, and tanks. They drove streetcars, operated heavy construction machinery, worked in lumber and steel mills, and unloaded freight. Rosie was powerful, patriotic . . . clever, competent. And, yes, pretty.

Canned goods were shipped to troops overseas. So, the government encouraged civilians to provide for the home front by planting Victory Gardens. *Life* and *The Saturday Evening Post* printed stories supporting the need. *Woman's Day* and *Good Housekeeping* printed "how-to" features. Twenty million Americans rallied. Victory Gardens were planted in empty lots, backyards, and even on City rooftops—all in the name of patriotism.

And on June 26, 1943, Howard M. Post's draft postponement expired. The short summer was over. He officially joined the nation's patriotic fervor.

Budd wrote in his diary . . .

> Good Morning: You're only young once! It was a great summer. Mom was "down" when she heard the news about me reporting to active duty. But I cheered her up with an encouraging talk to both Mom and Dad about the future. This is my last night at home while I am still the baby of the family—here's hoping I am starting on a brilliant career. One way or another, I'm off to Camp Blanding tomorrow!!

Camp Blanding's 170,000 acres were located six miles east of Starke, Florida, on the shore of the almost perfectly circular Kingsley Lake—some claim "The Silver Dollar Lake" is the oldest and highest lake in Florida. Its clear waters, sandy bottom, and 90-foot sapphire depth form the headwaters of the North Fork of Florida's Black Creek.

Camp Blanding framed Trail Ridge—the largest of several long, low, distinctive sand dune ridges in Central Florida. The trail's north-trending sandy sediments were eroded from rocks of the Appalachian highland, during the Pleistocene Quaternary. Some 20,000 years later, they remain as distinctive landforms in Florida's typically low terrain.

But Budd didn't go to Camp Blanding to enjoy Kingsley Lake or hike Trail Ridge. On July 6, 1943, Howard Malvern Post reported to Camp Blanding, Florida, to be inducted into the United States Army. (Only later did he learn that he was but one of 800,000 World War II soldiers to receive all or part of their training in Blanding's 10,000 buildings, at what was then the fourth largest City in Florida and one of the largest training bases in the entire United States.)

Budd, with *two* Ds, now *Private* Post, wrote in his diary . . .

> Good Morning—PV called and woke us at 5:40; at 6:10 we were eating waffles in the kitchen. We reported at the draft board at 6:30, and boarded the bus for Blanding at 7:45. It was a slow trip with several stops; finally reached camp about 8:00.

We got off the bus and were immediately started being "inducted." We were given instructions on how to stay in line, answer to our names, how to eat our meals, etc. We had supper first and then began the preliminary physical. We were ex-rayed and asked some questions for the record and at 11:00 we turned in, having been issued one blanket, sheet and pillow.

About 10:30 the guards began searching for Joe White—at 11:30 some wits were still hollering, "Anybody seen Joe White?" Finally go to sleep and did okay till 5:15 AM.

PS Sergeant Eddie Cohen is in charge of "Company X," the imaginary company for inductees. Mom's politicking helped—he was looking for me and said he could do me some good—my first sample of Army politics!!!

Up at 5:15 on this day and breakfast about 6:00. Soon after breakfast we began the physical. Stripped to the bare-skin, you follow the arrows on the floor for three complete examinations. I passed with everything perfect.

I had my choice of Army, Navy, or Marines when I finished. Naturally I took the Army. After that we had a mile-long bunch of papers filled out, and were assigned a serial number, and finger-printed.

Then we were told to report at 4:00 for taking the oath. Had lunch at noon, and supper at 4:00!! Then we were sworn in—at 5:30 PM, I became a Private in the Army of the United States of

America. At 7:40 we boarded the bus for home. They explained about things (the dependency allotments, insurance, furlough) all the way during the long ride home.

We made swell time until we got to West Palm Beach at 3:40 AM when we had bus trouble—it was 4:25 before we left, and then it was in a terrible old trap. We got out at 6:00 at 36ᵗʰ Street and the Boulevard. Caught the Hialeah bus and was sitting in the living room reading the paper when Mom and Dad got up. Now, I'll wait.

Private Post waited until July 28, 1943. Early that morning, Harry drove him and PV to the Hialeah train station, where they boarded the train headed to Fort Blanding and their *real* induction into army life. (Jeanne stayed home. She couldn't stand saying goodbye.)

The two best friends arrived at Camp Blanding at six o'clock, where they received bedding and were assigned bunks. Then, after a quick preliminary physical, Private Post was "turned loose to army life."

Trained and ready for action

Private Post wrote in his diary . . .

WOW! I'm in the army for sure. The company was divided up in details and we worked. I pushed a scrub broom through every tent in B Company. After dinner I scrubbed some more. We finished at 2:30 but unluckily some sergeant spotted us, and brother, I loaded a few truckloads of clay—regular ditch digging!

We went to mandatory movie for two and a half hours—it was quite interesting. Part was devoted to military courtesy and part to V.D. instruction—I'm sho' going to try to stay clear!

PV and I were assigned to Co. X. The duty officer informed us we were on the shipping list for Camp Fannin, Texas. I haven't the faintest idea where that is but the beauty of it is <u>we are going together</u>.

At 6:10 a.m., on August 6, 1943, Budd and PV boarded a train, and they were "on the way to Texas!"

Private Post wrote in his diary . . .

Spent a rugged night. PV and I slept more than anyone, but it still wasn't enough. The cars were old with no air conditioning. The windows opened and were soon black with dirt and coal dust.

Passed through Memphis, Tennessee—dirty and messy. We stopped for an hour but Beale Street was off limits because of race trouble. Sure wished I could have walked down that street. Saw the Mississippi for the first time. I enjoyed it greatly.

There was a captured German flyer aboard the train and he was answering a few questions— likes his treatment, food & thinks "America is very great." I couldn't agree more.

Come to find out, Camp Fannin was over 1,400 acres of woodland hills near Tyler, Texas, that the U.S. Government had converted to an Army Infantry Replacement Training Center and Prisoner of War camp.

The camp was named in honor of army Colonel James Walker Fannin Jr., a Texas Revolutionary War hero. It opened by Executive order in the spring of 1943. When it closed only four years later 200,000 men (sometimes as many as 40,000 at one given time) survived its rigors and became United States Army soldiers. Proud. Honored. Committed. After all, they *had* pledged, "This we'll defend to the very end."

Private Post wrote in his diary . . .

> Good Morning—My first day in Texas, and I think I'll like it here!

Private Post's experience at Camp Fannin was "rugged and strict." Although he liked Texas, his first few days in the army were "certainly not a piece of cake!"

Private Post wrote in his diary . . .

> Good Morning—Day One: Up at 5:30, revile at 5:45. Made beds; policed area. We were processed about 9:00—serial number checked, forms filled out, etc. After dinner we were given a G.I. haircut—boy, it's a dilly!! Then we were issued rifles—they were packed in cosmolene—greasiest things I ever saw. Cleaned them all afternoon. Then arranged all my equipment according to instructions, washed clothes, bought some stuff at the PX. No time to write letters. Damn.

Got stuck for latrine detail after breakfast. We had manual instruction all morning and more clothing inspection this afternoon and then retreat. Then cleaned rifle, shined shoes, etc. to get ready for inspection. After lights out had to hide in latrine to write letter to Mom and Dad.

Up at 5:30 and our cycle has begun!! At 7:30 we started in close order drill—1 hr.—calisthenics 1 hour—courtesy lecture 1 hour. Then mail call. I received my first letter from Dad—also contained dog chain, pictures, & clippings. After dinner fell in at 1:00 and after a lecture on military hygiene, we received some shots. It was extremely hot, and there were literally dozens who passed out— PV for one. There were also heat exhaustion and sunstroke cases in the infirmary. Then at 4:00 we formed in the blazing sun & dust and had an hour of gas mask drill—shee-yit!!! After supper (and I was feeling kinda' punk believe me) I had a special class on rifle assembly and nomenclature—we are going to act as "assistant instructors" in future classes. Then rolled a full field pack and fell in bed. Tired? WOW.

Up at 5:30 and another heavy day. After policing barracks we fell in at 7:30 with full field gear and had an hour lecture on clothing and equipment. Then an hour of pack-rolling instruction. Then an hour of calisthenics, during which about a dozen men fell out—heat. Then an hour of simple close hour. After dinner we fell in again and had an hour lecture on hand grenades. Then an hour of military courtesy. Then we formed in the theatre and heard different officers welcome us. Then a film on Army organization. After supper PV and I went to the PX and weighed ourselves—I weighed 121 & PV 132!!! Then to the day room to write letters.

Up at 4 AM to begin our K.P. I worked all day dishing vegetables, peeling apples, heaving crates, mopping, etc. Plus the job of personally washing 1800 pounds of spuds. Then washed 4 pair of fatigues, 4 pair leggings, and socks. Then had a swell bull session about old times until we hit the hay at lights out. Old times seem so far away. What a day!!!

Up at 5:30 and breakfast. Fell in at 7:25 and an hour of drill. Then some calisthenics; then saw a good "orientation" picture for the rest of the morning. Told us how, when, & where the war "really" began—Manchuria. This afternoon we fell out with full field packs, rifles, etc. Spent the entire afternoon learned field display of equipment and ran the obstacle course—rope climbing, cargo-net climbing and regular obstacles and two hours of hand to hand combat finished with an hour of close order. After supper had another class on M-1 functioning. Platoon had two hours of makeup work for the day. We had K.P.—military sanitation in the field. Lights went out with my rifle half cleaned. Then had bed check. Sure crowded me—was up till 1:00 in latrine cleaning rifle, shaving, etc.

Up at 5:30 and breakfast. Then hit two details before I could start getting ready for inspection— had to lay out every piece of G.I. stuff I had. I was very lucky—no gigs at all. If he had looked at my canteen cup—oh, oh!! (He did crawl me for having my leggings on under my sun-tans. I was trying to save time when time came to put on my fatigues.) Had drill and manual until dinner, and after dinner we had gas mask drill, aircraft identification, and a gas identification class. We cautiously smelled samples of war gasses. Two boys weren't careful enough & one began sneezing and the other was sick. After supper had another shot (feel like hell) and PV and I went to town to get undershirts, saddle soap, etc. Had a quart of milk. Then washed more mess gear and clothes for an hour or so. Fell into the rack at lights out.

My birthday. HA! After breakfast caught a latrine detail and then fell in for our first taste of gas. First we entered a building full of tear gas with our masks on. Then we were taken into the gas without masks and required to put them on inside out. Sick. Punk! After a class in defense against aircraft we were through. After dinner another 4 hours of PRI trigger squeeze and position. Got a letter from dad but no soap!! Spent all evening packing a full field etc. for tomorrow. WOW. Rugged. Strict.

This morning we saw another orientation film about Germany—propaganda. Then had a heck of an inspection. Was on the range firing at 8:46. My first impression was that the rifle made a heck of a lot more noise than I expected, and was very powerful. I fired a 37/40 prone, 38/40 setting during the day. After lunch we received new bayonets—they are much shorter and are sharp and pointed—rough stuff!! After supper PV hit a dirt shoveling detail so I cleaned our bayonets. The sky was pretty at sun-set and the sky make the sand have a weird, red glow. Also were paid to night—I got $35.50, much to my surprise, must send some home. Shined shoes, polished, cleaned—only to do it all over again the next day. Punk!!!

Up at 5:30 for chow. Then PT and a lecture on China. Then close order drill and back to the theatre for films and lecture on how to protect military information—fairly interesting but very simple. After dinner we began preparing for inspection. I was gigged for a little oil in gas chamber. Then Lt. Hawkins said, "Post! What branch of the service are you in?" . . . "The ARMY, sir!" . . . "Well, Private, get an ARMY haircut!"

Yes, Private Post was, indeed, "in the army now!" For the next three months, not much except the calendar page changed. Then, in early December 1943, Private Post was transferred to Baton Rouge, Louisiana, where he enrolled in Louisiana State University's Army Specialized Training Program.

Private Post wrote in his diary . . .

Good Morning—Jughead and I arrived in Baton Rouge train station at 5:30 AM. (Had my first champagne last night—tastes like piss-n-vinegar.) Two trucks carried us out to the U. It's a very nice place. After some "processing" and orientation we were assigned rooms. I'm very satisfied so far.

My first impression of L.S.U.: the campus is beautiful in places; the Mississippi River flows by a block from my window; A.S.T.P. [Army Specialized Training Program] is a disappointment—not enough discipline; lots of coeds; I miss all my old friends, No PX or Q.M.—laundry means more expense.

Went to the U.S.O. and met a couple L.S.U. girls—very nice. One of them is going to the Point for the Christmas formals—lucky gal! Coming home on the bus I got the name of a girl who is the best yet; I'll have to inquire further!!

Registered for classes—filled out a lot of the same forms that civilians would. We carry 35 hours of Engineering per week. Had my first revile with the whole company, and what a spectacle! They fall out in a snappy 15 minutes, or thereabouts! Nuts!

Got my books—Physics, Chemistry Lab, English, History, Geography. The Hist. Prof. is an excellent lecturer—enjoyed his class. The Geography Prof. is piss-poor—had a quiz in his class and might have "guessed" and still got 75%. He's a dried up weed! Messed up an analyst test, though—forgot a damn sign in a little formula. Skipped out of P.E. and think I'll get caught. PUNK!

Played poker after supper—won $1.75 all told. Even better got paid—drew $46 for the month. Sent $30 home.

This New Year's Eve 1943 is rather sad. I miss home and all my own friends and I miss Julia. Maybe 1944 will be a better year. I pray God will guide me and give me strength, and make it a happy New Year. Amen.

On March 6, 1944, Private Post was transferred to Camp Maxey—a World War II infantry training camp, located ten miles north of Paris, Texas, in North-central Lamar County's Red River Basin. Had circumstances been different, he *surely* would have enjoyed fishing for largemouth bass, white crappie, sunfish, and catfish in Maxey's 6,000-acre Pat Mayse Lake and exploring its15, 000 acres of surrounding woodland.

But Private Post (along with 43,000 other ground-force troops) was assigned to Camp Maxey to practice training maneuvers on its artillery range, brave its obstacle course, master its infiltration course, and conquer its "real" German village.

Private Post wrote in his diary . . .

Good Morning—Once again shipping day rolls around. We boarded trucks and were ferried to the same station through which we came in. We loaded 12 cars of troop train and moved out. It was a long dirty trip, and cold as heck trying to sleep. (The only happy part was a series of fortunate poker games!) We arrived at Camp Maxey at 4 PM and were met by the band and a big truck convoy. The assignments to companies was most peculiar—the first men walking together were assigned to a certain co.; another truckload somewhere else—just by chance I wound up with some good boys. Actually, the boy I bunk next to is from Miami Beach. George Orr, by name of Orr Construction Company—first Miamian I have met.

Days are typical—usually DULL. Up at revile and breakfast; PT for an hour and then rifle cleaning—good deal, cleaning our rifles on government time. Then parade practice and instruction in things such as gas, personal hygiene (including that messy film by "Gonorrhea Gus"), familiarization with the .45 pistol & bayonet practice, malaria control. Then, dinner. After dinner we endure more PT, practice falling out, learn about things like the mortar compass, military courtesy, discipline, map reading & articles of war. Then we hike and parade. After supper we wash our clothes, write letters, and if we're lucky play poker. Lights out at 10. We fall into bed. And Good Nite . . . until we get up to do it all over again. Dull. Dull. Dull. (Something that is NOT dull is Lt. Nowlin advised us to **make a will !!!)** Gosh, I'm really homesick.

Something interesting today—finally!! Usual parade then 3 hours of chemical warfare—smelling samples of war gases, gas mask drill and a VERY interesting demonstration of chemical grenades, smokes, incendiaries, and tear gas! They gassed us to see our reaction—we ran!

Then, if that wasn't enough, this afternoon we had 3 hours of dry fire and then bayonet assault course—pretty rugged. One boy fell and another almost mistook him for a dummy. There were several sprains and barbed wire cuts and 5 broken rifles within the company.

Had a good break today—was picked to go on a bayonet demonstration detail by Sgt. Oneida. After dinner we had 4 hours review of marksmanship and then retreat parade. Lt. Nowlin called me aside during position drills and asked my opinion of the men. He also said I had been on the ball and suggested I was in line for a rating in the future. (Lt. Col. Allan had asked me several questions in the previous period, which I answered right—that helped!!)

Worked hard all day. Finally had supper at 1930. Took a shower, cleaned my rifle, and started playing poker at 9:30. Was down $15 for a while, but finally WON $12.00. Hot Dog! (We played in the latrine until 0245!!!) Smoked my first cigarette last night riding the bus from town, and smoked about a pack tonight. That's enough for me.

Great day— Was in the fields on platoon tactics. Was appointed second-in-command during morning and had whole squad during afternoon, but we quit tactics after an hour—too bad. I'm good.

After breakfast we went by truck to a combat range and ran a squad attack problem—REAL munitions course. After dinner we ran the infiltration course—and gosh, it was hard on the elbows! We crawled about 100 yards on hard clay with the usual MG fire overhead. After supper we went back and ran the course by night—it was quite interesting because they fired tracers. We started back about 9:15 by truck, and then the fun started. Captain Goldberg stopped the convoy & made us walk <u>6 miles</u> back to the area. This was because <u>everyone</u> was making cracks about him. This was mainly because in his usual chicken manure manner he made Kyle run the course <u>twice</u> during the afternoon because he stood up a little too soon at the end. (We had not one word of instruction about the course.) We hiked the 6 miles in 80 minutes—singing part of the time. Sho' did feel good to have a hot shower & soft bed!

June 6, 1944—**D-DAY—!!!! The allies invaded France today. Nothing else matters!!!** President Roosevelt knew last night that the invasion was underway while he spoke to the nation and announced the fall of Rome. He said "One down, and two to go!" Personally, I was sick as a pup; my stomach was in terrible shape, and a headache all day!! I couldn't get out of bed.

It is now the 28 of July 1944—one year after I entered the army. To celebrate (I guess) I made sharpshooter, but my firing was terrible. Come to find out when I went to the service club someone else "zeroed" my rifle. What a joke!! PUNK!! Anyway, I'm an official Expert Marksman with an Expert Infantry Badge for M1 rifle and MKM rifle.

Wonder if I'll get to use it to takedown Japs??? Here's hopin!!

Quite a day! I was sitting in the half-track in front of headquarters and I accidently fired a blank. Naturally a Lt. Col. chewed my ass out and Major Matassa had someone take my place. Damn! After dinner another Lt. Col. chews me out for wearing white socks with low shoes—I had to read the AR's pertinent and change them— **CHICKEN SHIT!!!**

After about three months of "chicken shit" experiences at Camp Maxey, Private Post was reassigned to Cornell University in Ithaca, New York.

He wrote in his diary . . .

Good Morning—I thought I'd never get to New York. It was quite an experience driving through the City! But, anyway, here I am—cold, rainy, even light snow flurries. YIPES! Not liking this weather too well. The identical emotions which I felt at L.S.U.

Classes started, and I am beginning to enjoy it here. Heard a talk by Colonel Van Dusen, and he explained what was expected of us here, including which Naval officers did and did not rate salutes. ("For Christ sake, don't salute any G.D. anchors!!!")

Hurray!!! Letter from PV. He's overseas. Sure wish I was with him, but I guess it just can't happen. I'll make the best of it at school—enrolled in what's called the "certified course," and will take English (made the advanced class, sophomore level), Algebra, Physics, and History (political and diplomatic history from 1815 to present). I really like the physics prof. He is head of the Physics Dept. and author of the textbook. Smart guy!! Really swell!! (What rhetoric!!)

Stood in a half-ass reveille in front of Cascadella Hall this morning. Punk! The good news is I got results of my class tests. I'm leading BOTH sections. Yippee!!

Do you believe it? I got thrown out of Huck's class—"profanity." I said I couldn't understand which of the damn sides were which in the theorem concerning the side opposite of an acute angle. Damn. Remember my resolution to stop my damn cussing!!!

Well, this is <u>interesting</u> . . . I received a wire from Pepper [United States Senator from Florida] saying I had won his second alternate to the Naval Academy. What about West Point? A little history . . . I want to go to <u>West Point</u> . . . I took Senator Pepper's competency exam for <u>West Point</u> . . . I got my third alternate appointment to <u>West Point</u> . . . I took my <u>West Point</u> physical . . . I'm here at Cornell taking the damn "certified course" so I can go to <u>West Point</u> . . . But now the <u>Naval Academy</u>??? Punk!!!

[One month later] My official Navy appointment papers came today. I guess it's Annapolis for me. Durn.

In early January 1945, Private Post received orders to report to Fort Benning, Georgia. Okay. Fine. *Whatever.*

Private Post wrote in his diary . . .

> Good Morning—Not a good day—This morning we were informed that we had to move out of our rooms BY NOON so officers could have them. Man, were we P.O'd!! I asked the CO if that were true, and we had a real go-round. He threatened to court martial me for disrespect. Horse shit!!! Then after supper the real bombshell—We are all being shipped to Fort Benning, Georgia immediately after March examinations. We will receive the basic training generally given during "Beast Barracks." It suits me fine. I'm at the point of <u>whatever</u>—don't give a damn.

Fort Benning was an army post located in Southwest Georgia, just outside Columbus. Since 1918, it was known as *The Home of the Infantry.* Its mission was "to produce the world's finest combat infantrymen." And it did. Five star generals, Omar Bradley, George Marshall, Dwight D. Eisenhower. George Patton, and Colin Powell all trained at Fort Benning.

When Private Post arrived, in 1945, Fort Benning boasted almost 200,000 acres and billeting space for 3,970 officers and 94,873 enlisted personnel.

Private Post wrote in his diary . . .

Up at usual time. We got on busses and were carried out to Ferry Ridge. We spent the morning making a sketch of the area. Had dinner in the field (on paper plates mind you!) (Went through chow line twice—very good) and in afternoon we toured the Post studying aerial photographs. THEN we heard the news: President Roosevelt had just died at Warm Springs. I was stunned, but it is true. He died of a cerebral hemorage (SP). I hope Harry S. Truman will be the case of the little man lifted to great heights by his task— he'll need to be lifted!! No mail still, but President Roosevelt's death just overshadows everything!!!

Things aren't so bad here. Easy. Up at 6, reveille, chow. Then some map work and practice assembling the M-1—stuff like that. Had a formation this morning for Roosevelt's memorial service. It was okay, I guess, but could have been better. After lunch played a little basketball, threw the baseball a little, and got some sunshine and worked up a sweat. Took a shower and started to write some letters, when I discovered I had lost my money order from Mom. I called Western Union and was told that eventually I would get the money. Durn, I'm awful careless. Will have to do better. After supper a bunch of us went to Columbus to the USO dance. It was P-Poor.

A little excitement today—after dinner on the range we fired. I got hit under the left eye with the open end of a hot cartridge ejected from the gun on the left; it's lucky it wasn't any higher.

Then we had a parade. I carried the company flag. They awarded several combat infantry badges and several dozen good conduct medals to guys who, unlike me, are <u>REALLY</u> in the war. Boy, it was a long time to stand at parade rest.

Today is PV's birthday—thinking about him and all my friends who are "over there." This thought just ran through my mind: My "Good Morning" at the head of diary page is due to PV. When we were in H.S. we greeted everyone that way, regardless of the time of day!!

When I think back I recall going out one morning and getting the Miami Herald (I was in my pajamas) and telling Mom & Dad that Hitler had invaded the low countries. WOW was that a long time ago! And here we are today V-E Day! **The war in Europe is officially over!!** I am thankful, especially for PV and his folks.

Spent a busy day on the mechanics of the 37 & 57 AT guns. They had two large coke machines in the building! This evening I went to town with Olly & Murphy. Supper at Ralston Hotel and then to Phoenix City. What a bunch of dives. I'm almost ashamed I even looked over there, and I'm durn sure I'm not going back. Sent home $75 worth of war bonds—at least that's one way I can support the war. Think about it: PV is over there and I'm here getting gigged for (1) pocket being unbuttoned (2) no shave (3) sleeves rolled up (4) writing on helmet liner (5) non GI shoes. <u>PUNK!!!</u>

Played poker from 7:45 to midnight and it was a memorable game. I won $5, and in one hand of 7 card stud my first five cards made a ROYAL FLUSH!!! That's the first time I ever saw one, much less held one. Naturally the pot wasn't too large!!

Graduation Day! It was a beautiful night last night—bright moon. But listen to what happened to me. Was changing my clothes when the major walked in. "What are you men doing?" he asked. "Fu__ the dog" I answered not knowing who it was. ALMOST didn't graduate after that one!!! Anyway, fell out for graduation and marched over to theatre #8 and received our "diplomas." That's it?

Well, not quite. On July 24, 1944 I was discharged from the United States Army. Had a conference during the morning, mostly concerning jobs in civilian life—they didn't waste much time on me—the <u>soldier boy</u> off to the <u>Navy</u>. The only problem is Claude Pepper's office **lost my papers from the Navy.** What a bunch of nincompoops!!!

Eventually, Budd's papers were, "straightened out," and on August 1, 1945, he reported to the United States Naval Academy in Annapolis, Maryland.

In 1845, George Bancroft (then Secretary of the Navy) established what he called the *Naval School*, on the grounds of Fort Severn—a former army post. Year one, seven professors instructed 50 Midshipmen.

Interestingly (perhaps ironically) what was to become the United States Naval Academy was built inland because of the *Somers* Affair. The *Somers* Affair was an alleged mutiny of the navy's infamous USS *Somers* that involved possible pirates, pilfered brandy, merciless flogging, leg irons, murder plots, death by hanging, and ultimately, burial at sea.

Anyway, by the time Budd arrived, one hundred years later, the story was just a *story*. By then, "Navy" was a full-fledged service academy that lived its motto: *Ex Scientia Tridens*—"Through Knowledge, Sea Power."

Most likely, Budd and the other Plebes (first-year students) followed traditional Navy Induction Day protocol:

"I-Day" Schedule

6 AM—10 AM: Plebes check-in at Alumni Hall, where they are welcomed by command chaplain staff. Immediately following welcomes, they receive their first orders which are given quickly and sternly: "From now on the first and last words out of your mouth will be 'Sir' or 'Ma'am'. Do you understand?" (Plebes answer in unison, "Yes sir!") Plebes then surrender all civilian clothing and belongings.

6 AM—3:30 PM: Plebes rotate through stations in Alumni Hall, including vision screening, medical testing, drug and alcohol screening, the barbershop where they receive identical crew cuts, uniform fitting and issue, the chaplain's station, and the administrative station. Note: The Plebes are examined for tattoos and piercings. If any are found, they must be approved by a senior officer or the Plebe will not be allowed to attend the USNA. Before departing Alumni Hall, they receive their first introduction to the Academy's Honor System and are taught basic military courtesies, such as saluting. They then board buses and are transported to the midshipman dormitory, where they are shown how to mark clothing, stow equipment, and arrange rooms appropriately.

6 PM: Plebes participate in the Oath of Office Ceremony in Tecumseh Court and officially become Midshipmen. Oath is as follows:

> *"Having been appointed a Midshipman in the United States Navy,*
> *do you solemnly swear that you will support and defend*
> *the constitution of the United States*
> *against all enemies, foreign and domestic;*
> *that you will bear true faith and allegiance to the same;*
> *that you take this obligation freely,*
> *without any mental reservation or purpose of evasion;*
> *and that you will well and faithfully discharge the duties*
> *of the office on which you are about to enter,*
> *so help you God?"*

After the ceremony, Midshipmen formally sign their "Oath of Office" papers, which commit them to Naval Service. Weather permitting, Navy pilots then perform a fly-by.

6:30 PM—7:30 PM: Midshipmen may visit their families in Bancroft Hall. They will not be allowed to see their families again until Plebe Parents Weekend.

7:30 PM—9:30 PM: Midshipmen receive general military training in assigned company spaces in Bancroft Hall

11 PM: Lights Out.

Midshipman Post wrote in his diary . . .

> Was sworn in as ordered. Already I can see a lot of Navy ahead—maybe all my life. This afternoon I started stenciling the clothes I was issued. What a job! I only had 1/3 finished by supper—my first meal in a Navy uniform. Came back and tried to get a little order out of the mess. To bed at 11:00, tired, kinda' bewildered, but thinking I'll actually like the place.

Time passed, and for about six months Midshipman Post did "like the place." Then, in February 1946, the tide literally turned.

Midshipman Post traced the events in his diary . . .

> Went to my first drill—"Steam," otherwise known as Marine Engineering. Guess what! I'm glad that I came here instead of the Point! I'm learning Navy life, even though it is sho' slow.
>
> Reported to the duty boat to board the SWIFT. We got underway and the race was on. I enjoyed the run down, particularly when we hit a good breeze and went tearing along with the rail

awash! Got in Oxford about 6:45 and a swim before we went ashore. Some gal swam around the harbor and finally came aboard. One thing led to another & I dated her. We had several beers in the only "juke joint" in town and then some first classman told me I'd better shove off. He tried to take over but he didn't get far!! The trip back to campus was sad as hell. He and other wise showoff bastards got drunk and puked all over. They're a sad bunch of G.D. babies.

At supper formation in the mess hall they announced it "THE WAR IS OVER!!!!" [August 14, 1945] All hell broke loose. We banged on pitchers, trays, and what have you. Then the brigade congregated on the terrace and whooped, whistled, sang, threw toilet paper, painted Tecumseh, took pictures, and rejoiced in general. Academic work was cancelled for tomorrow and yard liberty was granted to all till taps. My first thoughts were that PV and others won't go to the Pacific.

At 11:00 we began a parade for General De Gaulle. He presented a medal to Admiral Fitch at a distance of 25 feet from me. I got a good look!

After chow Mom and Dad were in the rotunda as scheduled. It was swell to see them, but I must admit that I must be growing up; somehow it's different seeing them now than it was when I used to go home. We walked around the yard a little and talked a lot. I was surprised at their feelings about my resigning. They don't go for this Navy career stuff much.

After supper called home and PV answered the phone; gosh it was wonderful to talk to him, and it will be even better when we get together at Christmas.

Up as usual and off to chow etc. Called Mom after French class. My resignation is almost in the bag—in hands of authorities. I may be making a serious mistake but time alone will tell. I must confess I am a wee bit disinterested in the daily routine and classes, but am going through the motions.

[Two days later] Finally talked to Stocky & he convinced me. I'm withdrawing my chit. I'm going to stick it out—I'm not going to be a quitter. Still, I can see I'll never be a star here at NAVY!

Saw Navy beat Penn State 28-0 from the Press Box!!! I was spotter for Don Whitmire [football tackle eventually elected into the football hall of fame]; the beauty of the situation is that I may have the inside track on the job for next year; then I would travel with the team.

What a red-letter day this was! I was mate of the first deck and I really had trouble with the first class. I turned on a light and when I woke the reveille inspector he was really pissed. Went around at release and did deep knee bends for ten minutes with paper on my hands to keep me from going down fast. The last straw was "run the obstacle course before reveille tomorrow!" DAMN. But that's only the beginning, folks. After chow went around to another first/c bastard on the first deck & did pushups till I was beat, then more deep knee bends. Then more pushups for another guy for making too much noise. **Bastards.** My achin' legs!!!

Went sailing before breakfast until 12:30. The bay was rough as all hell. We took on a lot of water and it was right chilly. Another black day at Navy—until I got back and took a shower and by 2:15 was playing golf. Finally, **MY** game!!

Home for Christmas!!! My train got in at 2:00 in the morning and Mom and Dad and PV were there to meet me. It sho was wonderful to see him again—and I mean wonderful!!! Great to be home—went to the glades and found a 6 foot rattler on the Homestead Road off the Tamiami Trail with one button. So good to see my friends AND play golf—shot 79 but I won't complain. [December 31] I'm on my way back to the academy—DAMN IT!!!

Back at school only three weeks [January 24, 1946] and things are red hot—Dad wants me to come home immediately and start in business with him. My chit goes in tomorrow!!! But I'm kinda messed up now, after almost committing to stay. Such is life.

Good Morning: January 25, 1946. Red letter day—I handed in my resignation personally and saw it approved. I signed the official copy and started the practical arrangements. Good Bye NAVY. There are great changes ahead for Budd—but I can't exactly prophesize. I do know for the first time in my life since high school days, I'm home for good.

—∿∿∿∿∿∿—

"Home for good" started in February 1946, when Budd went to work for civil engineer, M.B. Garris. He worked until May 31, 1946, when he "quit his job."

Budd wrote in his diary . . .

> First day as a working civilian. Dad drove me into town and at 8:00 I reported to Garris's office. The day was interesting but not hard. The old man is pretty slow. We were surveying a lot just north of the 17th Avenue Bridge and the block containing Moore Furniture Co. Got paid and left at 5:00. $6.00 per day. I think I can make transit man for the old man if things work right. I bought a surveying text.

> Worked on Biscayne Key today—went by boat from Matheson's estate below Dinner Key. Enjoyed the work—it centered around the lagoon where they filmed "They Were Expendable." I'm getting a great tan!

> Off to the Keys for a week!! Important day for me—I turned my first angles. Apparently the old man has decided to make me his transit man eventually. I'm learning to double-center, turn angles, cut lines, and set great corners.

> Off to the beach this morning for a lot survey. What a place—3rd St. and Euclid—*oi! oi! oi!* After

work rushed to Flossie's wedding. I got the jitters just watching—I can't see myself in a similar setting.

But Budd's new civilian life wasn't ALL about work.

Budd wrote in his diary . . .

> Mrs. B. and I went to the races. Dad explained the principles of the whole works, and we lost $3.00 apiece, while Mrs. B. and Mom proceeded to win several bets including one in which their $2.00 win ticket paid $149.10!!!

> Bob Pearce and OB picked me up tonight and we went to the Green Lantern in the Gables to a Lambda Chi dinner dance. I took Bobby Lint and she wanted to get looped—so we did. Finally got home at 1:30.

> Sally, Flossie, PV & I went swimming in the lake. Flo and I managed to fall off Howardson's boat while half-dressed. Then went fishing and caught 3 small ones.

> Played 40 holes today—putted well and never missed a shot. PV gave me cuff links and a German side sword from his time in the *real* war. Still wish I had been there. But, oh well. The important thing, now, is PV is back and it's just like old times—almost.

> Dad and I qualified at Bayshore for the County amateur; what a round! Ruined my nerves on #1 when I had to walk back for two clubs I left. Then

on #4 five snotty little girls gave me a hard time. Finally scratched out a miserable 76.

Took Mom and Dad to supper at Jansen's and to see "Bells of St. Mary's" at the Olympia; the stage show was good—that Ingrid Bergman is some woman!!

Picked up Betty Jo at 7:00 and we had supper at the "New York Delicatessen"!!! I had pickled herring. Then wound up at "Tarzan and the Leopard Woman." YIPE!

This is VERY important: PV is my best friend, forever. SOOOO . . . Up at 5:10 and it was 42° F!! The coldest April day since 1915. PV and I left the Springs at 5:45 and breakfast in Homestead; picked up Rayfield at 7:30 (PV screwed up the detail a little, but he was driving, SOOOO) and off to "Madeira Hammock." Left the car at 9:30 and before 1:00 I spotted a deer. Got a thrill out of seeing him, my first wild one; was amazed at the size, brightness, and whiteness of the "flag" as he took off. It was wonderful. Perfect. There wasn't a cloud in the sky; it was warm enough in the hammock and cool enough outside to be comfortable walking. Saw a barred owl in the hammock. Had lunch under a tremendous oak tree; it must be more than 15 feet around the base; One limb runs out horizontally 50 feet from the trunk and circles completely around and back on itself forming a circle about 10 feet in diameter. It was in this oak that PV and I set our "nameplate"—a copper piece, 3 X 5, inscribed "PV and Post were here." **The Keys are for me!!!**

Budd and PV Everglades Explorers Christmas 1950

Budd continued surveying for Mr. Garris until June 1946, when he quit his job and registered at the University of Miami. Then, uncharacteristically, for almost two years, Budd rarely wrote in his diary. When he did, his entries were brief. Hurried. Frankly, not telling, or even interesting.

On May 31, 1948, Budd wrote in his diary . . .

Graduation Day—wish I had recorded it on time.

That's it. Not one word about his life at University of Miami. Only from Budd's diploma do we learn that *"The University of Miami upon the recommendation of the faculty has conferred on Howard M. Post the degree of Bachelor of Science in Engineering Science with all the rights, honors and privileges thereunto appertaining. The witness whereof, the seal of the University and the signatures of the President and the Dean are hereunto affixed. Given at Coral Gables, Florida on May 31, 1948."*

Jimmy says . . .

> *Dad never talked much about his experience at the University of Miami. About all I know is he was in the first class that graduated from its School of Engineering. Then, he taught night classes in surveying while he was working for the State Road Department.*
>
> *I think Dad always wanted to be an engineer. After all, when he was young, his dad took him to construction companies in Miami Springs that specialize in building foundations, driving pilings, and pouring concrete. After Dad saw what it was like in the rock pits, I can guarantee you he didn't want to do that.*
>
> *I can also guarantee you that while Dad was in school he didn't spend all his time studying. No way. He lived in an apartment on Le Jeune Road, in the heart of Coral Gables. Knowing Dad, he played golf and dated like crazy. His life was most likely big time party time!*
>
> *You know, Dad lived University of Miami's motto:* Great is the Truth. *He did great things for his entire life. And he demanded the same out of everybody who worked for him. Actually, he demanded the same out of everybody who was anybody in his life. So, I find it strange that after Dad graduated, he didn't support the university.*

Sure, he encouraged me to apply to University of Miami when I was applying to engineering schools, but he encouraged me to apply to every good engineering school. For some stupid reason, I chose North Carolina State. But a South Florida boy in North Carolina during the wintertime is another story.

I flunked out on purpose. So, Dad called up his buddy who owned a road construction company, and the next thing I knew I was laying road pipes. Well, it didn't take me long to enroll in Miami Dade Community College. Dad said, "You do a full year with a 3.0 average or above and I'll help you pick your college. In the meantime, if you get fired from your job, you're on your own."

Anyway, I am a big University of Miami fan. So much so, people always ask me, "Did you graduate from University of Miami?"

I say, "No. My dad did, and I just picked up where he left off!"

After graduation, Budd worked for the Florida State Road Department. (But that's another story.) His next phase of military life began in January 1949, when he enlisted in the United States Army Reserve, 841st Engineer Battalion, and was commissioned as a Second Lieutenant.

In 1908, Congress created the Medical Reserve Corps. Then, in 1920, under the National Defense Act, Congress reorganized United States' land forces by authorizing a Regular Army, National Guard, and Organized Reserve, which later became the Army Reserve.

The Army Reserve's mission is "to provide trained, equipped, and ready Soldiers and cohesive units to meet the global requirements across the full spectrum of operations." So, in May of 1951, when the 841st was called up to active duty and deployed to defend the United States of America during the Korean War ("Korea"), Lieutenant Post honored his responsibilities. Rapidly. Efficiently, Skillfully. No questions asked. After all, Army Reserve personnel are "always engaged." Korea was no exception.

> Prior to World War II, the Korean peninsula was part of the Japanese empire. After World War II, Americans and Soviets were left to decide what to do with their enemy's possession. In 1945, two young State Department aides divided it in half, along the 38th parallel. Russia occupied the area north of the line. The United States occupied the area south of the line.

Friend or Foe?

By 1950, two states had formed. The south was ruled by anti-communist dictator, Syngman Rhee. The north was ruled by communist dictator, Kim Il. Neither despot stayed on his side of the 38th parallel. Border skirmishes were common. Then, on June 25, 1950, some 75,000 soldiers from the North Korean People's Army charged across the dividing line.

This was not just another border dispute—United States dignitaries were convinced it was the first assault in the Communist's campaign to rule the world—a symbol of the global struggle between East and West, good and evil. President Harry S. Truman said, "If we let Korea down, the Soviets will keep right on going and swallow up one place after another. Inaction is NOT an option." Some even warned that without United States intervention, World War III was eminent.

So, in July 1950, American troops were deployed to defend South Korea. It was one of the hottest, driest summers on record. Desperately thirsty troops drank water from rice paddies fertilized with human waste. Intestinal diseases went from bad to worse. Fighting escalated. Casualties spiraled. Secretary of State Dean Acheson said, "If the best minds in the world had set out to find us the worst possible location in the world to fight this damnable war, the unanimous choice would have been Korea."

In July 1951, military commanders initiated peace talks. Negotiations stalled. Two years later adversaries signed an armistice. Some five million casualties (military and civilian) gained an extra 1,500 square miles of land for South Korea and a two-mile-wide demilitarized zone—border barrier—between North and South Korea. The Korean peninsula itself remained divided.

Lieutenant Post wrote in his diary . . .

> Incidentally (!!!) the last three days are filled with Korean War news; I feel that it is the first of an inevitable series of "incidents" and that the US's stand is the proper action.

> Went to Reserve meeting tonite. Not much as far as Korean rumors about fighting. But clearly the Army wants me for active duty. Read "The Naked and the Dead" till 4:30 AM. What a morbid, miserable story. But that's war. That's soon to be me. A peaceful man doesn't have much say-so or chance. Wasn't my usual sparkling self tonite!!! To

top it all off, these damn Parker 51 fountain pens are a pain in the you know what for diary writing.

Christmas Eve 1950—small, quiet party at the house. No particular emotions, except this is probably the last Christmas & New Year's at home for awhile. Expect the Army will have me next year.

This was D-Day! At the office this afternoon, Mr. Cullum came in and said, "Well, it's been nice knowin' you." And then explained that the 841st had been called for June 1, 1951 active duty. I'm off to Korea, for certain. Good!

Today was quite eventful—went over to ORC Hdqtrs. at the Armory to be sworn as First Lieutenant.

September 1952, Home away from home

Then . . . nothing. Budd does not write a single word about his experience in Korea. Not one.

The only intel comes from Bob Harris who reports that while Budd was in Korea, the 841st built the Kim Po airfield. And Jimmy who tells us that while Budd was in Korea, Harry Post ended his own life.

We can't ask Budd why he stopped writing in his diary. We can only surmise that 1951 was tough. Horrible. Heartbreaking.

On January 1, 1952, Budd wrote in his diary . . .

> 1951 was rather a disastrous year. Dad's death was a tragedy. He was a fine and gentle man, and I loved him. I grieve to think of the misery he must have suffered prior to his death—and especially the last hours that he spent so alone. May I emulate his virtues and avoid the pitfall into which he fell.
>
> Beverly's actions were also a bitter pill. She was married during the Christmas holidays, but not to me. Thus, endeth another chapter.

Then, on October 24, 1984, Budd wrote in his diary . . .

> Dad died 33 years ago today—and I can still re-live the moment Mrs. Balling turned the phone over to Mom—who told me—and my reaction—and Cpt. Marsh leaving me alone at the phone in the S-3 office in Ft. Huachuca—I put my head down on the desk and wept . . .

After Korea, Budd served as an Assistant Operations Officer in the Army School of Engineering, 841st Engineer Battalion. Again, Budd did not write in his diary. But Bob Harris says . . .

I met Budd in November 1956, when I was in the Army ROTC program at the University of Miami. I was a member of a group called the Persian Rifles, which was a fraternity of ROTC members. Budd came to the armory on a recruiting mission for the 841st Engineer Battalion to sign up ROTC members who had potential to become leaders in the 841st U.S. Army Reserve.

Budd was kinda' skinny but in great physical shape. With his blonde hair and dark eyes, I thought this Second Lieutenant Post, who was the executive officer of the 841st Company B, was a dashing officer with a very, very commanding presence. Still, I didn't sign up the first day he tried to recruit me. But when he came back in March of 1957, I signed on the dotted line—Budd had this way about him that made people want to follow him.

So, there I was an enlisted man in the Army Reserve. That meant in July of 1957 I had to attend summer camp at Fort Benning, Georgia. Well, the second week of camp the entire unit (we were a combat engineer battalion at the time) was sent out on bivouac—we pitched tents in the woods. AND . . . let the war games begin!

The company was split into aggressors and defenders. I was the acting sergeant of the aggressors. Budd and Lieutenant Colonel John Lindsay, who happened to be PBS&J's lawyer, were defenders, holed up in the command tent. Per protocol, the defenders were "smarter," "more experienced," "totally tactical." Still, the aggressors managed to infiltrate the lines and capture them. Boy, were they mad! No matter— everyone always enjoyed summer camps.

By the late '60s, Budd had been promoted to captain and was the company commander of Company B. (He was promoted to major a couple years before he mustered out.) But no matter what his rank, Budd was a great officer. He knew the Manual of Arms (how to march) by heart. Lindsay did not. And in the beginning, Lindsay was the commanding officer. So, when we were in battalion mass formation, marching along on the parade ground, Budd marched directly behind Lindsay, whispering commands in his ear. In reality, Budd ran the battalion from the beginning.

But that was Budd—he was an outstanding leader. I'd even go so far as to say Budd was a born leader. When he gave commands, we listened. We wanted to listen. We wanted to follow him. We trusted him. His voice had a commanding authority, and we knew he wouldn't say a word unless he absolutely knew what he was doing.

Ready to build it

Time passed. Eventually, Budd served as commanding officer of the 604th Aviation Engineer Battalion. Then on August 25, 1984, Major Howard Malvern Post retired from the United States Army.

Like his father before him, Howard M. Post was always and forever "a proud military man."

8.

Gentleman's Game

Golf.

No one knows how it started or even why it is called *golf.*

It could be that golf started in 1297, in Loenen aan de Vecht (the Dutch province of Utrecht), when Dutchmen played a golf-like game with a stick and ball.

Or, it could be that golf started in 1597, when explorer/ cartographer Willem Barentsz and his crew played "colf," as they traveled through Nova Zembla (an archipelago in the Arctic Ocean, in the north of Russia), searching for the Northwest Passage.

The crew's Officer Gerrot de Verr recorded in his diary . . .

> *Den 3. April wast moy claer weder met een n.o. wint ende stil, doen maeckten wy een colf toe om daer mede te colven, om also onse leden wat radder te maecken, daer wy allerley middelen toe zochten.*
>
> *(The 3ʳᵈ of April the weather was nice and clear with a north-easterly wind and quiet, then we*

made a colf [club] to play colf with, and thus make our limbs more loose, for which we sought every means.)

Another possibility is that golf evolved from the Roman game paganica (a game of the common people), when during the first through fourth centuries, players hit a small, feather-stuffed leather ball with bent sticks.

Then, there is the China versus Scotland brouhaha . . .

Chinese professor Ling Hongling, of Lanzhou University, claims he uncovered evidence of golf played in China as early as 945 CE, when a prominent magistrate instructed his daughter to "dig goals in the ground so I might drive a ball into them with a purposely crafted stick."

On another continent, 5,000 miles away, a spokesman for the Royal and Ancient Golf Club of St. Andrews claims, "Stick and ball games have been around for many centuries, but golf as we know it today, played over 18 holes, clearly originated in Scotland."

Scots go on to claim the word itself is a Scots alteration of the Dutch *colf.* (Webster contends the word is late Middle English but "of uncertain origin.")

Most likely, the disputes will never be resolved—or verified.

The rules of golf, though, are traced easily . . .

On March 17, 1774, Dr. John Rattray penned *Articles &
Laws in Playing at Golf,* for gentlemen golfers of Edinburg,
Scotland. There were thirteen. No charge.

(Twenty-first century golfers can buy a book. It's called
Rules of Golf. Two hundred pages. Twenty-five bucks.)

Articles & Laws in Playing at Golf

1. You must Tee your Ball within a Clubs length of the Hole.

2. Your Tee must be upon the Ground.

3. You are not to change the Ball which you Strike off the Tee.

4. You are not to remove Stones, Bones or any Break Club, for
    the sake of playing your Ball, Except upon the fair Green and
    that only / within a Clubs length of your Ball.

5. If your Ball comes among water, or any watery filth, you are at
    liberty to take out your Ball & bringing it behind the hazard
    and Teeing it, you may play it with any Club and allow your
    Adversary a Stroke for so getting out your Ball.

6. If your Balls be found anywhere touching one another, You are
    to lift the first Ball, till you play the last.

7. At Holling, you are to play your Ball honestly for the Hole,
    and not to play upon your Adversarys Ball, not lying in your
    way to the Hole.

8. If you should lose your Ball, by it's being taken up, or any other way, you are to go back to the Spot, where you struck last, & drop another Ball, And allow your adversary a Stroke for the misfortune.

9. No man at Holling his Ball, is to be allowed, to mark his way to the Hole with his Club, or anything else.

10. If a Ball be stopp'd by any Person, Horse, Dog or anything else, The Ball so stopps'd must be play'd where it lyes.

11. If you draw your Club in Order to Strike, & proceed so far in the Stroke as to be Accounted a Stroke.

12. He whose Ball lyes farthest from the Hole is obliged to play first.

13. Neither Trench, Ditch or Dyke, made for the preservation of the Links, nor the Scholar's Holes, or the Soldier's Lines, Shall be accounted a Hazard; But the Ball is to be taken out teed / and play'd with any Iron Club.

John Rattray
Captain of Golf
March 7, 1744

Golf in America is also traced easily . . .

In February 1888, a Scotsman by the name of John Reid and several other lads carried their wooden clubs and gutta percha—"guttie"—golf balls to a pasture in Yonkers, New York. (Tees were yet to be invented.)

There, on a three-hole course, obstructed by gnarled apple trees, in front of a gallery of confused cows, "The Apple Tree Gang" played a gentleman's round of "gowf." They tucked flasks of fine Scotch whiskey into knickers' pockets. They wore heavy tweed jackets, starched-collared white shirts, neckties, and tweed caps.

Scotch whiskey and proper attire aside, this was the first round of golf played at what was to become the oldest, most venerated, continuously existing golf club in America—Saint Andrew's Golf Club, Hastings-on-Hudson, New York.

Golf is a great game . . . fresh air, spectacular scenery, magical moments, community connections, family traditions, lasting friendships, business relationships, even physical fitness.

Why, then, did Mark Twain say, "Golf is a good walk spoiled."? Could it be golf exasperates and embarrasses, angers and annoys, players more than any other game known to humankind? Or perhaps it's because golf is a silly diversion, a serious vice?

Well, as Bobby Jones (the most successful amateur golfer, ever) once said, *"Golf is assuredly a mystifying game. It would seem that if a person has hit a golf ball correctly a thousand times, he should be able to duplicate the performance at will. But such is certainly not the case. Golf is the closest game to the game we call life. You get bad breaks from good shots; you get good breaks from bad shots—but you have to play the ball where it lies."*

Budd Post played golf for 75 years. He had good rounds, great rounds—trying round, terrible rounds. But wherever the ball did lie, when Budd was on the golf course, he was *always* happy to be alive.

Jimmy says . . .

> *It's safe to say Dad started swinging a golf club when he was eight, maybe nine, years old. That's when he got me swinging anyway. It was like father, like son. Dad loved to play with his dad, and I loved to play with my dad. Golf is part of our family's DNA.*
>
> *Still, Dad was smart enough to know I was a little hardheaded, whippersnapper who didn't take instructions well from him. So, he immediately got me lessons with Bob Toski, who was one of the greatest golf coaches in the history of the game. Dad and Bob were good buddies, so it was very brave of Dad to turn me over to Bob and trust me to behave. Great for me that I did. It was very good for my game.*
>
> *When I got older and slightly more mature, Dad included me in his regular golf games with his business partners and everyone. That was wonderful. Not many fifteen-year-old kids get to have that kind of experience. That was just one of the neat things about growing up as Budd Post's son. He took me everywhere—business*

meetings, jobsites, commission meetings, just hanging out in the office. I got to see a lot about PBS&J. I learned a lot. That was fantastic. It put me way ahead of the curve—WAY ahead.

Anyway, I'm ninety-five percent Irish. I have a real temper. So, when I didn't hit well, I banged clubs on the ground. Dad told me to stop. Well, as he got older and his game started failing, I'd tell him to stop. That role reversal is an interesting thing. But Dad was driven to be very good at the game for his entire life. During his heyday, he wasn't a guy you wanted to play in a throw-in, unless you wanted to lose your wallet.

The thing is Dad didn't talk about how good he was. I didn't know he won Jackson High School's state championship until I found the trophy. Then, I read the articles Dad cut out and saved and learned he won two state high school championships and then went on to the Biltmore Open, which is a national championship, and beat the reigning national amateur champion— just kicked his rear. Not bad for a sixteen-year-old kid who was playing with adults. I'm sure he was extremely proud, but he was never one to brag about anything, no matter what.

Dad loved the challenge of golf. Golf is the most frustrating game in the world. It is the most precise game in the world—the swing, the grip, the ball's direction are all very precise. And Dad was a very precise person. So, the game drove him crazy.

Dad loved to win. Dad wanted to win. When he didn't hit precisely and perfectly, he was very frustrated. He could get damn angry when he hit a bad shot, especially when he had something on the line like a dollar bet. But he never stayed mad long.

I remember the year I was thirteen years old I went with him to the Florida Engineer Society annual convention in Acapulco, Mexico. We stayed at the Acapulco Princess hotel. To Dad, the highlight of the convention was the hotel's two spectacular golf courses. One morning, he and I played. It was one of those rounds where he couldn't do anything right, and I did everything right. He tried like crazy to come back, but knew he was doomed. I beat him, and boy was he pissed. Eventually, he congratulated me, but the first words out of his mouth were, "You little shit!"

Grand Hotel Golf Course, Point Clear, Ala.

Happy moments on the links

150

*Dad loved the camaraderie—the friendships—
that is part of the game of golf. He probably
conducted as much business on the "nineteenth
hole" as he did in the office. But I have to laugh
because even on the "nineteenth hole" he was
competitive. He rolled the dice to see who was
going to pay for drinks. Dad rarely picked up
the check.*

*Dad was as frugal with golf as he was with
everything else. During the eighties, he bought
a new set of Tommy Armour 985s, made by
McGregor, through Bob Toski at Ocean Reef.
Dad played with those clubs the rest of his life.
Eventually, the groves were completely worn
off the sand wedge. But did Dad buy a new
one? Nah.*

*He always wore classic Izod shoes. He had two
pair—one black, one cordovan—and alternated
between them. He changed out the spikes but
wore the shoes until they literally fell apart. He
wore the same dark slacks and light-colored
pullover shirts—nothing flashy—until they were
faded and literally had holes. . Dad wasn't a big
spender on clothes, period. His closet held the
bare minimum—just what he needed. When Dad
went on a golf trip, he could fit everything into
one carry-on bag.*

*Dad's swing was as smooth as silk. Sure he
practiced to fine-tune his game, and every so
often he took a lesson to work out quirks, but
I'd say he was a natural golfer. When he was
younger, he was a scratch golfer. As he got older,*

his handicap was probably one, maybe two or three, consistently. He got off shots all the time. He was a machine! Smooth. Steady.

If there was a secret to Dad's success as a golfer, it was well-kept. Obviously, he was very good at math and had an analytical mind, and that helps with golf. Then, he was patient, and one of the greatest gifts a golfer can have is the ability to hit a shot, whether it is good or bad, put it out of your mind, and boom . . . move on. Dad could do it, and he taught me how to do it.

During the seventies Dad joined Riviera Country Club in Coral Gables and won the club championship for at least two years. Well, Riviera had caddies, so, Dad would take his caddy (he always used the same one) to the warm-up area and drop a small bag of balls. Whatever club Dad used the caddy knew exactly where the ball would land, so he'd go stand in that spot. And sure enough . . . Blam! Blam! Blam! . . . Dad landed the ball at his feet every single shot. It was unbelievable.

Dad's touch around the green was deadly— absolutely deadly. I watched him chip more balls in the hole than anybody I've ever seen. And his putts—well, he hardly ever missed, even the twenty-footers.

Dad admired Gary Player—the man dressed in black. One year, he actually got to play with Gary in the Doral Open. That was the thrill of his life. Then, he played in the Miami Open with Sam

Snead and Ben Hogan—all the greats. Years later, I saw an article saying Dad finished in sixteenth place on Saturday, but by Sunday afternoon he was ahead of Sam Snead. When Dad was just a sixteen-year-old kid, he even played with Walter Bonwit, of the Bonwit-Teller Bonwits. In 1950, he played in the Silver Anniversary Amateur Public Links Championship on the Seneca Golf course in Louisville, Kentucky.

Dad played in lots of PGA amateur championships over the years. During World War Two, he was the base champion at Fort Huachuca in Arizona. Even when Dad was in Korea, with a war going on around him, he played golf and won some big championships for the U.S. Government. No doubt, golf was his sport.

To tell you the truth, I think if it hadn't been for the war and the fact that back when Dad was playing golf, pros didn't make any money, he would rather have been a professional golfer than an engineer. But with the money pros make today, heck yeah, he would have loved it.

I know for sure he would have been very proud of our nephew, Harris English, for being such a successful golfer.

You see, golf was Dad's passion. I have a picture of him that was taken during a PBS&J tournament. He's sitting in a tent, after the round, leaning back in his chair, drinking a cold beer, relaxing with his employees. Dad has a big smile on his face. He's at the height of his success, *just having a ball. I never saw him happier to be alive than he was that day.*

Budd always aligned himself with the best of the best—for instance, Bob Toski. Tom Kite (winner of more than $2 million and two Vardon Trophy awards on the PGA Tour) says, "Bob Toski has long been the premier teacher in the game of golf. Most of what the majority of teachers are teaching today has been taught by Bob for a number of years. He's probably studied the golf swing as much as or more than any of the other teachers."

Budd and the Master, Bob Toski

Bob Toski says . . .

My memories of Budd go back to the late fifties, early sixties. He was a good player—a low handicapper. But there was more . . . Golf is a gentleman's game. A real golfer needs to think and act like a gentleman. Budd was a true gentleman. He had good self-control. I never heard him curse. If he did, he did it under his breath. He had a gentleman's attitude and demeanor. He was one fine golfer and a wonderful student. I really enjoyed teaching him.

Back when Budd was my student, people didn't talk about "this is my short game, or my long game, or my bunker game, or my putting." They just wanted a lesson from Bob Toski. So, I always started by asking them to hit golf shots, and I watched the flight of the golf ball—the tempo and rhythm, with the tempo being the rate of speed and the rhythm being the sequence of activity.

You see, there are only three absolutes in the golf swing: you swing the golf club, you turn your body, and you shift your body. Actually, swinging a golf club is an inverted C. I like to see the range of motion and the sequence of activity, with the body supporting the swinging of the arms, and the legs supporting the arms, while the hips and shoulders are turning.

When you see that sequence and it is well controlled, it's like watching a great dance team. But that is difficult to do, and it is even more difficult because you must then find the ball, with the clubface square and consistently drive it toward the target. Budd had all those attributes. He was intuitively and instinctively that good at swinging a golf club.

After the swing, I looked to see what type of ball flight my student had—was it a draw or a fade, or a straight ball, or a low or high ball? If you are going to be a good, or even a great player, you must be able to control the ball up, right to left, left to right, hit it straight, hit it high, or hit it low. A player must understand the technique and then do it. Unfortunately, golf has changed and that's not how the game is being taught today. It's more of a power game.

Anyway, I don't recall any real weakness in Budd's golf game. Every part of his game was very consistent. If you're going to be a scratch player, you must be consistent in all departments. I remember so distinctly that I enjoyed teaching Budd because he was such a great ball striker. He had excellent form. His swing was orthodox, not unorthodox.

Still, I had to warn him about not being too mechanical. He was a typical German—almost too mechanically oriented. I always said that you need to play more by touch and feel. There's no substitute for touch. An ounce of touch is worth a ton of brawn.

I remember playing with Budd at Ocean Reef. Lots of guys get all pumped up when they play, but Budd's personality was of the demeanor where he was very quiet and easy going. Still, he was very competitive. He did not like to lose. He and I were very much alike in that respect. I won because I didn't want to lose. I do believe lots of players are afraid to win.

The game of golf is about inner drive. You force yourself to perform better. You test yourself as an individual. In competitive golf, you are one man against a field of a hundred and thirty-five to a hundred and fifty players. You play four days against Mother Nature. I always said, "I'm not trying to beat the field. I'm trying to beat the golf course." Unfortunately, I didn't see Budd play competitive golf, but I am confident he would play the same as I did.

For six decades, Budd recorded his good rounds and not-so-good rounds in his diary . . .

Budd's First diary entry about golf . . . Sunday, January 8, 1939

"Brite & Fair"

Went to Sunday school today and while Mom was in church Dad, Bingle & I went over to the course and hacked away a bucket of balls. Came home and did Susie (homework) and Good nite!!

Later in 1939

Went and played 18 holes and shoot 91, shot my first legitimate birdie of my life and shot my lowest score, on an easy course.

1940

Played golf all day long. Putted & played 9 holes in morning—46. Practiced woods & 42 again aft. Had a par on #1. Hitting my woods lots better. PV and I went over to the golf course tonite & "Bunked a few Bunkers."

Went to club and putted a while. Then Dad and I started to practice & while we were so engaged Dad popped the question about "being good." Told him the truth. Never again. This afternoon played with Mobley & two other guys. Lost $1.50. Won't be a sucker anymore.

Met Stubb after school with members-to-be of golf team. Then had play practice and eased myself out of the play—I want to play golf!! Came home, hit a bag of golf balls at Willie Daub's, cleaned clubs, and oiled bag and cleaned my new Winchester .22—Hot Dog!!

Team played Miami Hi—Tolmadge & I took all 9 points in our match but the other guys fizzled. I was putting like a house-a-fire.

Played golf this afternoon. Shot a 79!!! Had supper went to movie—it was punk. Came home & have caught hell every other minute . . . I drive terrible; I sulk; I have a long face; I'm discourteous; I'm bold & so on ad infinitum.

Qualified in Glenn Counters tournament with an 85. Beat Dad even for the first time!! He had a 91.

Went to banquet at beach. Was awarded my cup for winning the sixth flight—may it be the first of a long line of cups. Oh yes, the first draft number was picked today (October 29, 1940). I'm #158.

Went over to Biltmore and played 45 holes in one day—the most I've ever played, so far!!!

1941

Went to golf course right after breakfast and Jacobus started in on me. I thought I was stroking the ball pretty well—that my form was okay, but Oh Boy! I do not have enough firmness in my body. I sway & wiggle too much; I'm too loose. Lessons all morning.

1942

School was punk. But, oh, yes, I'm captain of the school golf team. Mom took me over to Biltmore and I played a round of golf with Dad. Dad gave me a general going over about my attitude, etc. Played fair on front: 38 and then played back nine well—35+73. That's one under for the second time in my life. Think & Think & Think & Remember the Resolutions!!!

About 10:30 am went over to Springs and hit some for about an hour. Then over to Biltmore and lunch. After lunch met Thuffy Cox and we decided to play off our match. Larry Tailer and Wallendorf played along too. Won $2.00. Also won the Miami Biltmore Mens' Handicap Tournament, 1 up in 20 holes. Boy, I really had to fight, 3 down going to eleven, even going to fifteen, 1 down going to #16, all even to #17. Into the canal on #17 while trying to play safe!! One down to #18. Had a 10 footer on #18 for a bird to square the match, made it!! Won on the 20th with a par.

Up about 6:45 again and went out to golf course. Had a good round in the morning—38-37-75, 3 over and played last two holes in 3 over! That gave me 6 strokes on Bryan. In afternoon had a terrible front nine—46 & lost 4 shots. Had 39 on back & gained one & won tournament with 318. Bryan had 321. Clyde was 3rd. Started for Fort Myers about 6:00. Went to bed about 11:00.

Played 36 holes today, and won $10.50 but then lost it back to Dad—NUTS!!—Somehow or other I can't hold my temper when I play with him—and naturally it hurts my game. Someday I'll get over it!!!

PS

Accomplishments today:

- ✓ Won high school tournament
- ✓ Played fair under pressure, but gained a load of experience
- ✓ Completed some trig
- ✓ Read Bible

PPS

Remember your revised resolutions!!! . . .

- ✓ More church, **less cussing**, and better Christian—confession of faith—with Dad & Mom—observe the 10 Commandments better
- ✓ Waste much less money
- ✓ Continue to drive very carefully

- ✓ Work hard at everything I do—don't be a quitter—<u>golf,</u> <u>school,</u> <u>Riflery</u>
- ✓ Due to breaking wedge today, I vow to try to control myself at all times, particularly on the golf course, & to especially <u>avoid cussing</u>
- ✓ Don't bet
- ✓ Behave myself, generally
- ✓ Keep clear of **all girls**
- ✓ Help me this day to keep my damn nose out of other people's business

Dad & Stubb & I played golf at Indian Creek—cost us about $34 to play over there. Had a good time—played 45 holes. I had the best round of my life in the morning—one over 73—with **SIX** birdies!!! I hit the ball beautifully—never in my life have I played so well from tee to green—hit <u>every</u> green.

1950s

At 5:00 pm, PV, George, Murphy and I played the front nine at the Springs. It was the best golf I ever played! I birdied #3, #5, and #6, and missed putts under 8 feet on #4 and #7! On four (!) out of the nine holes, I thought my second shorts were going in the hole (#4, #6, #7 #9! Finished with 32 blows!

Played golf today at Fort Lauderdale (at 0730!) and our "team" lost to the district office "team". I had a 37-42 for a 79.

Played golf today at Sea Island and it was quite a round. Played alone, pulling a cart, in 95 degree temperature, and had an even par 72! Holed out a 9 iron second shot on the second hole for an eagle! Played the two "old dunes."

Played golf with Whitworth, Colin Dixon, and Blackie Berthune at Miami Lakes. Had a 75 with first nine one under par! Was really hitting tee shots, but not much putting.

Played at Redlands with Ralph Jordan, Lew Whitworth and a Pennsylvania friend of Ralph's, had a 73 with 3 consecutive birdies on the front nine!

Played first nine at Miami Lakes today with Jimmy—gave him his new clubs as a birthday present and he had 73 counting them all, as they lie. I had 39 from the back tees.

Played golf with Ace, his college roommate Fr. Bob Murphy and Walter Revell. Jimmy drove the cart—I caught a green snake on the 6th tee (Blue) (Doral) and Jimmy kept him for a pet—what a hazard.

Jim, Bobby Ludwig, and I played the Par 3 course at Miami Lakes this afternoon and Jim had 71, with a hole-in-one on #8!!! And I didn't see the actual stroke. I was picking up a forgotten ball!

Was at Ocean Reef today—played golf in the afternoon with Bob Toski. Toski had <u>29</u> on front side. No freaks—just perfect golf!

It must be Saturday

1970s

Played 9 holes at Ocean Reef and was even par on the back nine, started birdie, birdie. Then played 6 holes with Beth Stone . . . and she won!

Played golf in Miami Springs Day tournament— had a 76 and won low gross. Jim, Mark, PV and Tim Phillips played behind me, Bob Hurt and PV. Jim had a 101—which was great if he didn't forget any!

Played golf at Rivera with Jim Scott, Vernon Turner and Buckley and played very poorly—81.

163

Teed off at 0745 playing with Dick Smith, Lenny Hinds, and Bob Bonner. Had 35-35-70, and that was good enough to be UC Champ!

Played in first annual FES Open, with Bill Watson, Bob Alligood, and Ernie Carlton and started 3-3 (back nine) which was birdie-eagle! Finished that side in 3 even par and then was 34 on front nine. Won the trophy and two dozen balls and am converted to Titleists now. I think maybe I do hit hard enough to use them.

Played in the Pro Am at CC of Miami—teed off at 9:10 with Judy Kimball, George Russell, and Evelyn Kapit—she is the wife of the guy who runs the Desk Center, where we bought the first desk for PBMS! Had a real good round—72—but we played from the ladies tees!! Putt out and drove very well.

PBSJ Golf Tournament Day!!! Jeanne took me and Jim to Kendale Lakes about 1000. I teed off at 1100, finished at 1600 and had to hang around till 1900 for everyone to finish, award prizes, etc. I was low gross (77). Jim had 90, which wasn't bad for strange course, 3 water penalty shots, and not playing for months.

1980s

Bob and I played Charlie Largay and Paul Herald at noon time and we won 1 up. I played one of the best rounds of my life—hit 14 greens

164

in regulation and had 11 birdie putts under 18 feet! Didn't putt several times because Bob had already holed out, but would have had 73+/-.

Went to Rivera for golf, played a threesome with Buckley and Buscaino and had 69!! 4,2,4,3,6,3,5,4 and 4 for a 35 on the front and 3,4,3,5,4,3,5,2 and 5 for a 34 on the back. Twenty five putts!

Had breakfast with Bungle and then golf at 11:00, played with George Buchman and Ed Russo. My new Ping irons came in yesterday, so I used them for the first time, along with Jim's metal driver with an 8 degree loft! Had 76 and was low net amongst the 16 payers (7 handicap). Hit 4 greens and putted very well (and chipped well too), including sinking a 12 footer on the last hole for a 4 that won the money—a good day!

Played George Dacy today in the semi-finals of the Riviera Club Championship—40 years after we played against each other in high school—he at Ponce, and I at Jackson!!! I won 2-1, but we both played terrible; I bladed 3 trap shots to cause me all kinds of trouble, although I hit the ball solid most of the time—but also missed an 18 inch putt and put a pitching wedge second shot on #12 in the trap! Was really charged up when I got home—ran 5 miles! Woke up at midnite and have been up for 3 hours doing bookkeeping etc.!

Daylight Savings Time Today—SWELL!!! Ran 5 ½ miles this morning before church and my left knee is stiff. This afternoon watched the Legend of Golf—Snead and January were 22 under par for 54 holes! Bob Toski sank a 10 foot birdie putt on #18 to tie them for second—a $10,000 putt!

Went to Boca Raton and took a lesson from Bob Toski at Camino del Real, and then played 18 with Roy Barden, who made all the arrangements with Toski . . . The lesson was simple: Shift your weight! I am inclined to reverse pivot—which gives me the cut-across, too much access-the-finish-line.

Tony and I played the #1 and #2. I played Jim Chaffman, a retired IBM executive, who lives aboard his yacht at Ocean Reef. We won handily, but the really freakish part was this: On #17, I had a hole in one! I used a choked 1-iron into a strong wind. But while we were on the green, Father Hudak (Tony's former parish priest) came up on the golf cart and told Tony that his (Hadak's) partner—named Herrera—had aced both #6 and #9!! That was 3 aces on the same course, the same day, two by the same guy, and he was playing with three priests!

Having a hole in one ain't no big deal, believe me. While Herrera's feat was acclaimed around the world, I paid for drinks at the 19th hole. Swell.

1990s

Golf at 11:00 with Overholt and McKinnon. We won the four ball and I won low net with a 78 (-7) = 71. But it was dissatisfying because I took 6 on #16 when I sculled another sand shot out of the right hand bunker, just like I did on Wednesday and 3 putted #18 for another 6 (double bogey) which mishaps (mental) probably cost me the over-65 medal! (82-78).

Played golf at noon with Jim Scott and I vs. Jim and Gary Dagnan. I had 80 (with 3 double bogeys!) and the match ended even. Jim hit some tremendous drives, but played very erratically otherwise from lack of play. (We are both 10 handicaps now.)

Went up to Ocean Reef for a short time, early, to try out the new driver that Jeanne gave me yesterday—a surprise! It works remarkably well. This afternoon late went over to Miami Springs Golf Course and hit a bucket of balls with the new driver. The 9 degree loft is amazing. I hit shots off the turf with that club that went better than if I was using a 2 iron. I don't understand it, but will pursue it!

Golf at Riviera at 10:30 with Buckley, Tony Macina, and Earl Courtwright, had 81. And also discovered my handicap has gone down from 12 to 11. I suspect our weekly scorekeepers are using a sharp pencil! I'll be more watchful in the future because I don't think I am playing any better than I have for the last year!!

Then, on December 12, 1998, Budd Post wrote his last diary entry about golf . . .

A do nothing day—because my aching shoulder and back ruled out golf. (I tried to hit balls at Riviera, but no soap.) Was home all afternoon except half-hour putting at M.S. Supper at Drug Store~~~~~~

9.

Better and Better

A wise, wealthy, wily man once said, "If you haven't found it yet, keep looking. Don't settle. As with all matters of the heart, you'll know when you find it. And, like any great relationship, it just gets better and better as the years roll on."

Budd wasn't a techie. Most likely, he never read Steve Job's advice. Still, the all great minds syndrome was alive and well.

Jeanne tells the story . . .

> *It took lots of years, and Budd and I went through lots of people, but once we found each other it was right and as years passed, it got better.*

> *I graduated from Mercer University—a Baptist school in Macon, Georgia—in 1945. Back then, girls, even girls with college degrees, didn't have many career choices. So, when I heard Delta Airlines was hiring stewardesses, I decided to apply.*

Delta started out in 1924 as a crop duster outfit that attacked boll weevils (small beetles that eat cotton). About 1929, Delta started carrying passengers—one at a time. The passenger got along fine, as long as he didn't mind riding in a straight chair, in a bin, where the pilot stored pesticides.

During the thirties, Delta carried more and more passengers and got larger and larger. Then, in 1945, after they added a route between Miami and Chicago, they doubled in size. Lucky me, Delta needed stewardesses.

Mother and I rode the bus to Atlanta, where I, along with lots of other girls, interviewed. I happened to write on my application that I was a member of Alpha Delta Pi sorority. As it turned out, the chief stewardess was a member of the same sorority. She didn't even ask me many questions. I was hired and that was that. Lucky again.

But that's where my luck ended. Let me tell you something . . . I would not take that job today. NO WAY. Back then, I thought it would be glamorous. The problem was I had never even stepped one foot on an airplane.

Our winter uniform was a plain navy blue suit and white blouse. Our summer uniform was plain beige. No pants. Always skirts. Outside the plane, we had to wear a small, unattractive, overseas cap. If we got caught without our cap, we got demoted. There was nothing—not a thing—glamorous about our uniforms. And it certainly wasn't glamorous when passengers upchucked on them—and back when I was flying, passengers upchucked more times than I want to remember.

We flew in DC-3s, made by Douglas Aircraft. They were small, so stewardesses couldn't be over five-four or weigh more than a hundred and fifteen pounds. We had to weigh in every month. And if that wasn't bad enough, the head stewardess slapped us on the butt to make sure we were wearing a girdle. Not glamorous.

We got paid a hundred twenty-five dollars a month, for every hundred hours of air time. That didn't include ground duties, which raised our actual hours to one hundred fifty. There is nothing glamorous about working fifty unpaid hours every month.

Anyway, most passengers were nice. Pleasant. And Delta gave us free passes to travel anywhere on its routes. I regret now that I didn't go to Europe, but I did go to Canada, South America, and lots of places in the United States.

I was based in Miami, where I shared an apartment with another stewardess. She was dating and practically engaged to Bob Schuh, who worked at a local engineering firm. (At that time, the name Bob Schuh didn't mean anything to me.) One day my roommate said, "Bob's best friend is a guy by the name of Budd Post. Would you like to double-date?"

I wasn't much for blind dates, but I wasn't busy that night so I said, "Okay. Why not?" So, they introduced me to Budd. He had light blondish hair and blue eyes. I thought he was a nice-looking man.

We went to see a movie starring Audrey Hepburn. To tell you the truth, I can't remember the name of the movie, but I do remember I'd seen it before and thought it was good. You see, when I first meet somebody, I'm not much of a talker, which is why I wanted to go to a movie. (Naturally, I didn't tell Budd I'd already seen the movie.)

Anyway, Budd and I hit it off right away. From the very first date I knew things were right between us. It wasn't any big whoop, but we were compatible. We felt right about each other, and . . . well, it's hard to explain but everything just seemed right.

I was thirty years old, and so was Budd. Other guys had asked me to marry them, and Budd had lots of girlfriends before me. But, you know, that was the past. We found each other. We knew we were meant to be together. When it's right, it's right. We weren't willing to just settle for someone else.

Budd and I met the day before Thanksgiving in 1954 and were married the following May. And until the day he died, fifty-four years later, it just got better and better. (In case you're wondering, things didn't work out for Bob Schuh and my roommate, but they sure did for Budd and me.)

Budd was not particularly romantic, but he was, well, nice. I don't remember him getting down on one knee and proposing. But I do remember he gave me his mother's diamond engagement ring. Years later, I looked at my hand one day, and my ring was gone. I looked everywhere, but I but never found it. Budd was very, very understanding. He even offered to buy me another ring. I didn't want another ring. It just wouldn't be the same.

Anyway, we got married on May 14, 1954, at the Presbyterian Church, in Miami Springs. Before the ceremony I tiptoed around the church, looking out every window, because I was afraid Budd wouldn't show up. He was nowhere to be seen. I panicked. Then, my bridesmaid told me Budd was with the minister in his study. All I could think was, Thank God he's here. The wedding will go on. I can't begin to tell you how relieved I was.

The beginning of a great marriage

Our wedding wasn't fancy. At the time, it was fashionable to wear a short, white wedding dress, so I went along with it. I had a maid of honor and three bridesmaids. The maid of honor wore a blue dress, and my bridesmaids wore yellow dresses. My cousin, who owned a flower shop, sent me my flowers. Budd wore a black tuxedo.

Our reception was outside at the Miami Springs Country Club. Nothing special—just the usual cake and punch. We went to Tower Isle in Jamaica on our honeymoon.

When we checked into the hotel, I said to Budd, "Remember to write 'Mr. and Mrs.' on the registration form." I didn't want him to forget we were married or, even worse, have the clerk think we were there on an illicit rendezvous.

After Budd completed the registration form, the clerk said, "I've NEVER seen such perfect handwriting." From the time Budd was a little boy, he had neat, beautiful, perfect handwriting. I guess it's because he was an engineer, but I've NEVER seen anything like it.

When we returned from our honeymoon, we moved into the house where Budd grew up. By then, his mother was a widow and didn't want a big house, so she gave it to us. We were lucky, because it was a nice house on the lake. And that's where we lived for most of our married life. I'll never forget the address: 871 Lake Drive, Miami Springs, Florida.

Budd worked as a district chief engineer for the Florida State Road Department and made enough money to support us. I'd had enough of my "glamorous" job, so I stayed home and was a housewife. You know—cleaned, cooked, made sure my husband was happy—all the things women did back in the fifties.

Budd's mother never allowed him or his dad in her kitchen, so he never learned to cook. That was fine with me. I learned to cook when I was a stewardess and lived in an apartment. The finest steak available only cost seventy-nine cents a pound. Budd was a fisherman, so we had plenty of fish. Steak and fish—pretty good grub for newlyweds, don't you think?

Budd drove a State car. I drove the Plymouth he bought after he got out of the army. Gas cost twenty-five cents a gallon. I bought our food for less than ten dollars a week. We didn't have a mortgage payment. So, we were in good shape moneywise—not fabulously wealthy, but we had a nice living and got along well.

I was born and raised Baptist, and Budd was a Presbyterian. But to tell you the truth, I was so glad to be with somebody who went to church I switched and became a Presbyterian—Baptists and Presbyterians are a lot alike anyway, so I fit in without any problems. Budd was very active in the church—church officer, deacon, and eventually an elder. I taught Sunday school for sixteen years. Like with everything else, our church life was easy—meant to be.

Married life, in general, was natural. Budd traveled some, but he didn't work long hours and was home most evenings. I tried to play golf with him, but I was so rotten I gave it up. He didn't care. You know, we just didn't have problems. We didn't quarrel or even fuss at each other. We just didn't.

Budd and I wanted children, but shortly after we got married I had a ruptured abscess on my tubes and ended up with a complete hysterectomy.

Budd described Jeanne's experience in his diary . . .

When I arrived home today Jeanne was doubled up with endometrial pains. Called the doctor and rushed her to Hialeah Hospital, pain, fever, tubal infection, all on top of endometriosis attack.

0500: Cold chill; pain increasing

0800: Dr. Rudnik: Take her to Jackson—bed available at 1100

1130: Arrive Jackson; pain unbearable

1500: Headed for surgery—in shock from burst abscess

1730: Surgery complete—odds 50-50

Jeanne continues . . .

Fortunately, I recovered, and we decided to adopt. Budd and I went to the Children's Home Society and insisted that our child would, eventually, be smart enough to go to college.

One day, the social worker called and said they matched us up with a birth mother, who was a straight-A college student, and it was time for us to look at the baby. We looked through a window. And there he was—our son. After our very first look, we told the social worker we wanted to proceed with the adoption. And you know what? Our son ended up being smart, too!

Anyway, our son was about three months old when we brought him home. Budd liked the name James. That was fine with me, as long as his middle name was Howard, after Budd. I didn't want some oddball name. I wanted him to have an ordinary name that he wouldn't be ashamed of. James—Jimmy—Howard Post is a nice name, don't you think?

After Jimmy was placed in our home, the social worker came by every so often to evaluate us. So, even though Jimmy was born February 9, 1958, the adoption wasn't official until June 17, 1959. It all worked out just fine. I sure wasn't going to let them take Jimmy back. No way.

And the family is official

You know, people always ask how it feels to be the mother of an adopted child. How does it feel? Well, it feels good. The child is your child, same as if you carried him for nine months. I'm very lucky to have my son. We had fun together as a family. Jimmy was an only child. Still, we tried not to spoil him.

Budd wrote in his diary . . .

Jimmy went to school today after missing a week with the chicken pops. Sure am glad he's back to normal, but he's got to get over the privileged character treatment he got while sick!!

Jimmy's birthday today so we took him and Susan to the zoo at Crandon—the first time for all of us. To commemorate the event, Cecilia the camel gave birth to a baby camel, sex undetermined.

Taking a few days off work at office—Church, Sunday school, read the paper. Worked on sprinklers and cleaned out the garage. More work on Jimmy's tree house today. Installed the firemen's pole alongside the tree house, and it was a huge success!! Jimmy spent the night with Mom and Jeanne and I had supper at Robin Hood, on our way to Jr. Woman's Club Frolics. The Frolics were interesting but the crowd was a collection that did not jive, as far as Jeanne was concerned. I'm enjoying this vacation.

Home all day except for a trip to Sears to buy Jimmy new Keds. Swam in Jester's pool with Jimmy. Jimmy loves that!

Went to Jean Crook's ranch today with Jeanne and Jimmy, Buck, Mo, Tommy, and Mark. We rode over in two jeeps, had picnic lunch, watermelon, etc. and home about 5:30.

Went fishing today with Capt. Gene Lowe Tavernier—me, Jimmy, Jim Glass and Ode Cox. Was hot and calm, but we raised two sails and Jim Glass caught one—got it to the boat—and it got off! It was almost dead tho—so I jumped overboard, swam to him, and gaffed him— dragged him to the boat! What a fish story!!!

Jimmy Says . . .

I'll admit up front that I wasn't always the easiest kid in the world. I got a few well-deserved paddlings. Then, the summer I was fourteen, Dad sent me to live with the Jernigan family, hoping they would straighten me out. Who knows, maybe they did. Maybe they didn't. I do know it was a great summer.

Regardless of my, well . . . hard head, Dad and I were close. I went everywhere and did everything with him. From the time I was in diapers, he let me drive the boat. I learned to be independent and how to get along in this wild-wild world. I was damn proud to be his son.

Budd wrote in his diary . . .

Big flap with Jimmy—he got bumped down to the slow reading group, so no more TV until reading & arithmetic improve. I love to read. HE should love to read. Currently reading "We"—Lindberg's book, which Mom had preserved since 1930! Also found "Buddy Jim" in the old trunk—the book Dad used to read to me when I was a baby.

Early church and Sunday school and played 9 holes at Doral late in the afternoon—Jimmy behaved <u>terrible</u>. Jean went into Hialeah Hospital at 2000 to have two moles removed in the morning. Jimmy straightened up the house when we got home—to make amends.

Went fishing this morning—Jimmy would have been with me except he behaved badly yesterday, so he was denied the privilege.

Drove down to Cliff's house today, and briefed him on some things for the Commission meeting. Had lunch at his house—crawfish salad that was delicious. Had Jimmy with me all day. Need to show him the ropes.

Early church today with Jimmy, then I fixed sandwiches for lunch while Jeanne taught Sunday school. About 1130 left for the boat—Jeanne, Jimmy, and two of Jimmy's friends. Cruised around the bay for 3 hours—let Jimmy drive. Returned via Bear Cut to the ocean and thence in the Govt. Cut and bay, it was rough on the outside!

Up early and took Jimmy fishing in Niles Channel and vicinity of Spottswood's island—watched a 10-foot thresher shark chase a 60# tarpon up on the flats and chop him in half right in front of the boat.

Jimmy and I got up early and had breakfast and went to Carol City High School to look at some defective drainage sumps. Then home by 0930.

Today was Pinewood Derby Day for the Cubs—our entry didn't get past the first heat, but next year we will do better. We learned!

Up and off to the Keys with Jimmy at 0700. Set a TBM at the water's edge on our own wharf—Jim was the rodman—his first time—10 years old. And thence to Lowe's to get the boat. Went back to the property, read the tide, and took soundings every 200 feet of channel, out 1600 feet. Then fished and caught 8 snappers at Dry Rocks, swam, and home about 6:30.

Jimmy continues . . .

For as long as I can remember, Dad made sure I respected hard work. When I was twelve years old, he had me pumping gas, twenty hours a week, for a buck an hour. You see, Dad's friends owned a gas station, with two bays upfront and a four-bay shop in the back. My friends and I hung out there, and I loved working with my hands. So, Dad said, "Alright. Fine. Get to work. Now!"

I worked hard, but there were perks . . . the soda machine had a blank button. Come to find out, the blank button vended cans of Miller High Lite.

I hit that button more times than I can count—thirty-five cents for an ice-cold can of Miller was a damn good deal.

I'll never forget the year Dad bought me my first bicycle . . . One day I forgot to lock it and someone stole it off our front porch. Dad said, "Lawnmower's in the garage. Five bucks every time you mow the lawn. After you earn enough money, you can buy yourself another bike."

Budd wrote in his diary . . .

Bought Jimmy a "Stingray" bicycle with a banana seat for his birthday. He was as thrilled as he can get. After supper took him to Sears to buy a padlock for the bike and bought a Cub Scout key chain & neckties, and a Cub Scout handbook.

Chores this morning—bought Jimmy a basket for his bike and was amazed to find that he had gotten the necessary tools out of my tool box and had it perfectly installed when I returned a short while later.

Well, it's a year later, had a little birthday party for Jimmy. Got him his new bike—a "5-speed." He had to earn it. After lunch and ice cream and cake I took the whole gang to Miami Drag Way, but it got rained out—heavily.

Jimmy continues . . .

Then there was the retainer lesson . . . I loved to play baseball in the park in front of our house and didn't want to be bothered by my retainer. So, I took it out. The problem was I forgot where I put it. Well, retainers cost seventy-five bucks. Expensive. So, after I lost it the second time, I got the same lawnmower speech, only ramped up. "Lawnmower is in the garage. Get your butt out there. And, this time, not just in OUR yard, but EVERY yard in the neighborhood." Dad wasn't about to buy me another retainer. No way.

Dad knew how to teach a lesson—real quick. Nothing—NOTHING—was delivered on a silver platter. Dad instilled a work ethic and a respect for earning money. His message was this: "Don't be foolish with your money. If you screw up, fix it yourself."

Dad also taught me about determination. He was determined, no matter what. When I was thirteen years old, we worked on Waterside in Key Largo (but that's yet another story), and he let me drive back to Miami Springs. Well, we always stopped at Alabama Jack's, where Dad bought a can of Busch beer. Dad liked his beer. But the day I got my driver's license, he quit cold turkey—never drank a drop again. That's determination.

Budd wrote in his diary . . .

Rev. Hunter preached today on "From Whence Cometh We" and the children's sermon was on habits and how they are weak when they start (one thread easily broken) but grown strong thru repetition—a rope is many threads. Been thinking about my dad's alcohol problem. For

184

Jimmy's sake, I don't want that to happen to me. So I quit drinking any alcohol today, until I am satisfied I am not dependent on it, as a habit.

The perfect match

Jeanne finishes the story . . .

Budd and I were married fifty-four years. In looking back, I honestly can't think of any problems—we just agreed on things. I was happy. Budd was happy. I admired Budd. Respected him. He made friends easily. Everybody liked him. He was a born leader—a man's man. If he said he was going to do something, he did it.

And he treated me well. VERY well. Budd had old-school gentlemen's manners. He always opened doors for me, and until the very end, he treated me like the true Georgia Southern Belle I am.

As I said, our life together just got better and better.

10.

PBS&J Corporation
Model for Many

"The success of PBS&J Corporation is a direct result of continuing to live our strong company culture and staffing all of our offices with passionate professionals who are focused on the needs of our clients. Our journey continues to be focused and guided by a series of standards that have established how we conduct our business and build professional relationships, now and in the future.

Mission: To provide professional services to our clients through technical excellence and innovation.

Core Values: Belief in the virtues of integrity, hard work and loyalty; relentless in the pursuit of quality and excellence; honor our promises and contracts; belief in open, honest respectful communications; actively support our professions; and personally invest in our communities.

Services: Investigations, Studies, and Reports; Cost Estimates and Feasibility Reports; Surveys—Boundary, Topographic, Hydrographic; Design and Supervision of Construction; Contract Administration; Municipal Consulting.

These services are offered in the following fields of competence: Streets and Highways; Bridges—Movable and

Fixed; Water Supply, Sewage Disposal, Airfields, Drainage; Land Development."

Howard M. Post
John D. Buckley
Robert P. Schuh
Alex M. Jernigan

Weighty words. Respectable. Responsible. Most companies make similar statements. What, though, is the story behind them?

It all started around 1948, when Budd Post worked in Dade and Broward counties, for what was then the Florida State Road Department (now, the Florida Department of Transportation, or simply *FDOT*).

For over ten years, Budd designed bridges, water and sewer systems, and roads in Florida. For instance, as resident engineer for the Miami Expressway System, he supervised over $35 million in highway and bridge projects. He was the chief engineer for the Golden Glades Interchange, where U.S. Route 441, Florida's Turnpike, the Palmetto Expressway, SR9, and Interstate 95 come together in Miami Gardens and North Miami Beach, Florida.

Budd and Bob Schuh's home building adventure

Bob Schuh says . . .

> *After Budd returned from Korea, he graduated from the University of Miami's school of engineering, passed additional examinations, and became Florida's 4,627th registered professional engineer. (I am Florida's 4,423rd registered professional engineer.) Budd, then, went to work for the Florida State Road Department.*
>
> *Around 1953, Budd and I created a partnership to build new houses—by hand. Our first project was a house in Plantation Key. Budd loved the Florida Keys. He loved to fish. So, this project was the best of both worlds.*
>
> *We made payments on a lot in Plantation Key and drew up plans for our house. It was a small cottage, built on stilts to protect it from high water during a hurricane. We'd go down on*

weekends and do a little here and a little there. Then, we'd stop construction and wait until we could save enough money to buy more supplies. Let's just say, like Rome, our house wasn't built in a day—we started in 1953 and finished in 1958.

Concurrently, Budd and I bought a third interest in a small, outboard fishing boat. We'd load equipment into our boat at Dinner Key Marina and start out through the mangrove swamp, swatting our way through swarms of mosquitos. Sometimes our motor worked. Many times it didn't. So, we'd row and spend the day fishing— another reason our house took so long to finish.

Budd wrote in his diary . . .

July 1, 1948—Thursday—and a red letter day at that. Up at 6:30 and off to Fort Lauderdale to begin work at the state road department. My first step after being shown to my table was to check my supplies, etc. I examined one gadget, which appeared to be some kind of a seal, or stamping machine; I was wrong. It held an ink bottle, which I promptly emptied into a drawer. After mopping this up, I began to get organized. Was put right to work plotting intersections on the proposed new super-highway, No. 9. The day passed quickly.

Back at the Miami to Battle Creek job again! 90¢ an hour, five nights a week, 6:00 to 10 PM. Makes a tight schedule at supper time, but it works.

QUITE A BIRTHDAY! At work today was informed of a $15 a month raise—making it $240 now. Ordered a new car—a green two-door Plymouth. Put up $200 cash and the jeep—monthly payments $76.18. Went from the office and hit a few shots with my new irons—fine! Truly a good day!

Worked exclusively on the Golden Glades road this past week. Tried a different approach to "the boys," since my "drive 'em" attempt only earned me a "chicken-shit" reputation. I just let 'em work at their own sweet-ass pace. It produces almost the same amount of work with much less effort and ulcers. Where is their motivation???

Mr. Cullum has turned over to me the job of preparing for construction at Golden Glades & Old Dixie Highway, which means getting squared away with the water, gas, and telephone companies. The telephone company is the problem. AT & T's main north-south coaxial cable runs along the East side of Old Dixie, and that thing has to be really handled with gloves!!! Rail strikes are beginning to tie things up; union officials say they are "powerless." The bastards don't believe in union responsibility.

Schuh and I messed around all day in the Keys; no fish; no crawfish; no sunburn; wonderful time. Drove down as far as the Toll Bridge around Plantation Key & Largo. Had a large BS session after chow, and finally home about 11PM. Note: Cash on hand $34.08.

Budd Post and Bob Schuh were not destined to go through life as underfunded, part-time builders whose livelihood depended on a dilapidated fishing boat.

Senator Bob Graham says . . .

In 1921, my father Earnest "Cap" Graham came to Florida to be the resident manager of a very large sugarcane plantation. You see, Dad grew up in Croswell, Michigan, where one of the primary economies was sugar beets. As happened, he became acquainted with people from the Pennsylvania Sugar Company, and they were looking for someone to run their large sugarcane plantation in South Florida.

Dad had never been to Florida. Still, he agreed to go down and write a report. The sugar company people liked his report so much they fired their resident manager and hired my dad. Then, in 1932, the Pennsylvania Sugar Company folded. So, as part of Dad's severance, they gave him dairy cows and approximately three thousand acres of pastureland on what was then the edge of the Everglades. That is how my father and my family got into the dairy business.

Well, as the town moved closer and closer to Dad's farm, it became clear that he could not stay in the dairy business, at that location, for perpetuity. Dad wanted to sell the land and move the cows to a location around Lake Okeechobee. But my two older brothers, Bill and Phillip, believed that because the land was so near a rapidly growing urban area, the family had a unique opportunity to develop it. Dad agreed.

So, my family started to look at new mixed-use land developments in North America and Europe. Before long, we discovered the New Town concept, which is an official category of land use. We studied the New Town concept as it was used in England during the interwar period and learned the English government's goal was to reduce population growth pressures around large cities, such as Birmingham, London, and Manchester.

The English government, then, established, developed, organized, and administered a series of self-sufficient towns that decongested larger industrial cities and rehoused citizens in planned communities. These English towns had all aspects of complete communities. They were places to live, work, recreate, educate, shop, worship.

And that New Town model was my family's primary inspiration to create Miami Lakes and the Graham family's contribution to a more orderly development of suburban areas in South Florida.

The Graham family's decision was well thought out. Perfect, actually. So, family members decided to move forward and purposefully plan, develop, and build what most likely would become overcrowded, congested, and, frankly, unattractive prime land in South Florida.

1948 / Off to work at S.O.D.
Dist. Office, Ft. Lauderdale.
(Started at $225/month) WW II Jeep.

The legend starts here

Now, the Grahams needed an engineer extraordinaire to execute their vision.

Bob Schuh says . . .

> *By 1959, Budd and I had pretty well decided our house-building venture wasn't such a great idea. Well, as luck—or fate—would have it, Budd knew Andy Cappelletti, who was on the Board of Sengra Development Corporation (former Florida Senator Earnest Graham's company). At the time, they were looking for an engineer*

to develop what is now Miami Lakes. So, as a measure of Budd's engineering prowess and integrity, Andy recommended Budd. One thing led to another, and before long Bill Graham approached Budd with a job offer.

The problem was the Graham family wanted Budd to quit his job at the road department and work for them. Well, Budd was an entrepreneur from the get-go. He had spent more than enough time working for someone else, especially a government agency.

State work was too mundane for Budd. He had too much energy, too many brains. He was too passionate about getting things done. So, Budd, great salesman that he was, simply sold the Grahams on a new plan: He would form his own engineering company, and they would hire him and his "associates" to do the work. The Grahams accepted his offer.

And, just like that, Howard M. Post (and *associates*?) was responsible for planning and building Miami Lakes—Florida's first New Town.

Now what?

Budd didn't miss a beat. He needed *associates*—engineers who could complement his highway and bridge expertise—engineers who had extraordinary skills—engineers he could depend on. And he needed them right now.

Budd contacted his good friends—Bob Schuh (structural engineer), George Mooney (general engineer), John Buckley (sanitary, water, and sewer engineer)—and offered them an opportunity.

Bob Schuh continues . . .

> *Budd had a way about him that was, well, convincing. It didn't take long before Mooney, Buckley, and I were onboard with Budd's idea to create our own company.*
>
> *The three other guys were married. I was not. So, THEY voted and decided I should quit my day job. I did. And that made me the first official employee of what was to become PBS&J.*
>
> *We threw in a hundred bucks each, and on Leap Year Day, February 29, 1960, Robert Schuh & Associates was off and running. (By year end we had lost money, which meant we each had to come up with another twenty-five dollars, which meant we had capitalized our venture for a grand total of five hundred dollars.)*
>
> *Anyway, shortly thereafter, we started work on the first hundred and forty acres of the Miami Lakes project. After we stabilized in 1961, the other three guys quit their jobs, and after a couple more iterations of our name, we became Post, Buckley, Mooney & Schuh. (Budd was the catalyst, so his name was first. Being the last guy in alphabetical order, I moved to the back of the bus.)*

Budd wrote in his diary . . .

March 7, 1961—Last day with SRD. Jim Deen, on behalf of the SRD employees presented me with a Benrus, self-winding, waterproof, dust proof, calendar dial, stainless steel watch & band! It was exactly what I wanted and had been looking for. Jim didn't make a flowery speech—just that "it came from the heart" and it kinda got me. I am proud of that watch and what it stands for. Now I'm off to talk to Billy Graham.

Worked all day and every night this week—hard!! Finally wrapped up the plans and specs for the sanitary facilities for Sengra's first development. Contractor started picking up the plans this afternoon. Our first big design job is more or less finished.

Realize I gotta' get out there. SO . . . Lester Collins is in town today; met with him and Bill Graham—steaks at Bill's house at 7PM. Lester (of the Cultural Landscape Foundation fame) is a fellow alumnus of the Harvard crowd, who runs the administration in Washington. I'm afraid he is a typical politician. The culture is overwhelming, but the practicality ain't there, nor is the horse-sense. Anyway, it was quite an experience to be present at a party with people who are on a first-name basis with people who are on a first-name basis with the President of the U.S.! (Graham is the magic name!)

Had dinner at the Top of the Columbus, as guests of the Grahams. The dinner, the view, the service, etc. were excellent. Met several new people important to Miami Lakes. A fine evening, which Jeanne and I both enjoyed, although she couldn't talk because of her laryngitis!

Miami Lakes going well . . . talked to Bill Powell today re: our inspection of ML construction. I explained there is no apparent reason to inspect anything but the water and sewer construction because those are the only portions for which we will have to certify that they have been constructed in accordance with plans and specs (to State Board of Health) except for seven (only) houses in Miami Lakes that are being FHA financed and will therefore require certification. Bill concurred with the position I took and said that they would inspect Miami Lakes just as any other subdivision. We will bow out, eventually.

Post, Buckley, Mooney & Schuh rented a single room, in a strip mall, at 225 Westwood Drive, in Miami Springs. Basically nothing. The engineers and draftsmen worked on drafting tables in the back; the bookkeeper sat at an old desk up front.

But Post, Buckley, Mooney & Schuh wasn't about office space. From the beginning, the four partners were, well, *partners.*

Bob Harris says . . .

> *I joined the firm in 1962 to work on the Miami Lakes project. The first thing I observed was how well the four founders worked together. One*

wasn't the "boss" over the others. If they had conflicts, no one else heard about them. Ever.

Budd wrote in his diary . . .

George G. Mooney became a full time active member of the firm today—July 17, 1961. He is already hard at work. The wheel has come full circle—in 1947, I went to work as an instrument man for George and Chelsie Senerchia, when they were partners, with their office at 43rd Street on NW 7th Ave. Now George, Buckley, Schuh, and I are partners. Feel real good today—better than in weeks.

The original team L to R: Schuh, Post, Buckley, Mooney

Bob Harris continues . . .

Friday night was beer night—a ritual. Guys went to the store, bought beer, came back to the office, sat around, and chewed the fat. Then, Budd said, "Okay, guys, hustle." And they did—we all did. And whenever someone did something especially well, Budd said, "Cream always rises to the top."

Anyway, the four partners divided roles and responsibilities . . .

George Mooney was a fine, fine engineer. Simply excellent. Probably the smartest design engineer I ever encountered. He had lots of experience. Before he joined Budd and partners he led the team that surveyed Tamiami Trail—the southernmost two hundred and sixty-four miles of U.S. Highway 41 that crosses the Everglades and forms part of the northern border of Everglades National Park.

But as far as personality, George had none. Zero. He was an introvert. He didn't like people. Most days he didn't even like the world. His designs were perfect. But when he finished, Budd explained them to the client. If we put George in front of a client, we wouldn't have a client!

Anyway, eventually, George retired because of heart problems. He was a good guy. We missed him.

Then, in 1965, Alex Jernigan became the fourth partner, which is why, in 1970, the firm ended up being called PBS&J.

Alex Jernigan was a fine engineer, and a self-proclaimed happy-go-lucky guy who enjoyed life and enjoyed people. He mainly developed business and worked on building client relationships, which led to PBS&J's expansion outside of Florida.

John Buckley was in charge of production and did a superb job. He was a very direct, hands-on supervisor. John was on his feet all day long, walking from desk to desk, standing over you, asking you questions—"Why did you put that pipeline there instead of over here?" If he wasn't happy with your work, he didn't hesitate to chew you out. He was a real bulldog around the shop.

Bob Schuh worked as a project manager and did administrative tasks—finance, legal, banking. He was a very demanding guy. Quiet. Detailed. He'd walk, from his desk, down the aisle between the drafting tables, to get a cup of coffee. And from "a mile away" he'd spot a misspelled word on your drawing.

Then there was Budd Post. Budd was a superb engineer. Precise. Brilliant. A perfectionist. Still, he chose to be in charge of marketing, which put him in the spotlight more than the other partners.

Budd was a natural leader. Charismatic. Honorable. You wanted to follow him, because if you did he would make you a better person.

Budd wrote in his diary . . .

> Attended last class of Mgmt 665 at U/M. Glad it's over, but the experience was valuable and worthwhile. For one thing, Dr. Shuman [Budd's major professor] convinced me that I am not a suitable candidate for an MBA –"Do you <u>really</u> want to be a student, or do you intend to act like an executive—the leader that you are?" I picked the latter.
>
> Still I had some professors I liked—admired. Dr. Holmes was one.
>
> Yesterday I felt depressed and filled with a sense of foreboding—like something bad was going to happen. Woke up feeling that way. Then about 8:00 this morning the phone rang—and I was scared it would be Jim with bad news about Jim; however it was Frances Holmes, and the news was bad—that Dr. Holmes died yesterday.
>
> I think this is the first time in my life that I clearly had a premonition of death or tragedy. Dr. Holmes death was difficult, but it was infinitely easier to take than had it been trouble, illness, or worse with Jim, Kerri, or the children.

Bob Harris continues . . .

When you asked Budd a question, you got your answer RIGHT NOW, and it was a short answer. He wasn't ugly. He just didn't see the need for extraneous conversation.

Budd wrote in his diary . . .

Frank Hogan, Chairman of Monroe Planning Commission, called at 0800 asking me to come to Marathon for lunch! I went and we discussed the Master Plan and how to implement it. I told him cold turkey how he had gone wrong.

Presented our proposal verbally to Ruiz, Chief of Planning, and Don Louis Montiel, Chief Engr. for bypass project and they seemed to like it very much. I proposed to prepare the Engineering Design Report for the project, which is where they are now, rather than final plans as they stated in their letter. Enough said.

Gave Ocean Reef the itemized bill for PBSJ services performed during January and told them that it had to be paid on or before they receive the next bill, or else we will halt ALL work until paid! Then I walked out.

Alex Jernigan says . . .

During the course of the day, Budd was usually out of the office. He was in Monroe County or somewhere else politicking with municipal or county officials. (To generate work, Budd HAD to press the flesh.)

But before Budd headed out, he came into the office, stood at his drafting table desk, and within an hour, he had handled ten things—sent them off to wherever they needed to be. By nine o'clock his desk was perfectly clean, and Budd was gone.

Budd wrote in his diary . . .

Busy day, but that's my life now. Finished administrative tasks in office. Then . . .

✓ Met with Hugh Langford, Ted Soady, and Mr. Hummell (President, RH Wright, Inc,) at 0800 to discuss Colombia. They are interested. I am to send a "brochure."

✓ Met with County Plat Review Committee at 1000 to present Miami Lakes Section One. Upshot was a suggestion by Stockhaven to submit for official action as tentative plat.

✓ Met at 1600 with Floyd, Bob Graham, Larry Johnson, to discuss water treatment plant for Miami Lakes I. (Johnson is a loud mouth promoter, but I gotta' do it.)

✓ Talked to Mr. Wearner of Canaveral Realty Company at 1800 about handling the engineering for their land development at Cocoa. We are to submit a proposal for feasibility report.

✓ <u>Note to self:</u> Hialeah Zoning Board, Hialeah Council, County Commission,

County Zoning submission deadlines are due "40 days prior." Gotta' get on it!

✓ To bed about midnight. Then, up and at 'em bright and early again tomorrow morning.

Flew to Key West on 0800 flight for Air Sunshine and the round trip fare is now $50, when it used to be $24, when there were two airlines (and gas a lot cheaper). **Saw**: Joe Allen re: water de-sal plant at Stock Island and employment leads for his son; **Saw** Claude Gehman about Stock Island water from garbage and water for N Key Largo Beach; **Saw** various other County officials, including Purie Howanitz, who is scheduled to become mayor tomorrow, after they oust Schlasir. Back on 3:00 flight. **Then** joint Deacon's meeting tonight; gave strong pitch for PV and new leadership for Camp Everglades. Bed around 1 AM.

Alex Jernigan continues . . .

Budd wasn't an outwardly missionary type of person, but he conducted himself like a Christian. Sure, he cussed the same as all of us. He drank whiskey the same as all of us. Then, he went to church every Sunday. I think that came from his mother. She was a redheaded, fireball. Whenever "Mom" marched into the office, everything got real quiet. We put our heads down and got to work!

Budd was as honest as the day was long. He lived by the Golden Rule. In the engineering business, you are approached frequently to do things that aren't legal. But neither Budd nor PBS&J followed that model.

Budd wrote in his diary . . .

> Commission wanted a deal. No soap!!—no matter what it might mean for PBSJ. Explained 7 + 1 = 8, and 8 + ½ = 8½. always, no matter what!!

> Board meeting was interesting—surveyor's bill was the most heated topic. Had hearing on Al Webber license revocation. Excused myself because he is working for DOT on Keys bridges—including PBSJ work.

Alex Jernigan continues . . .

> *Paying off politicians is a good example of what politicians ask engineering firms to do. Budd wouldn't have any part of that. I'll never forget the day Budd and I went to lunch with the mayor of Miramar, Florida.*

> *The mayor said, "Budd, I want to ask you a question. Let's say you designed a job for the city, specifying that the steel comes from the United States. Then, you later learn you can get the steel from Japan, which means it would cost less, which means the contractor could use the benefit to pay off the city councilmen. Would you do that?"*

> *Budd didn't blink. "No."*

The mayor said, "Then I don't have a problem hiring you."

PBS&J didn't want any part of a project that didn't have the highest standards. There's an old saying, "If you get in bed with a skunk, you'll end up smelling like a skunk."

Anyway, back then, city engineers were totally different than they are today. PBS&J handled everything—sewers, water, streets, paving. The city hired us on a continuing basis and whatever the city needed, we did it. (Today, the city's staff is very involved.) We kept many of our clients for better than twenty years, without any problems whatsoever. We were partners. Running mates. Brothers. There was no limit to what we did in the way of engineering for our cities.

The best way to describe it is to tell you that we were excellent citizens. We built personal relationships with the people in our cities. And when you build personal relationships, one thing leads to the next, leads to the next, leads to the next. You never know when, where, or how your relationships will show up. But you can be darn sure they will never abandon you.

Budd wrote in his diary . . .

Took time away from office work today just to have lunch at Ocean Reef with County Commission, Zoning Board, assorted other officials, and all the muscle in Ocean Reef Club, Inc. Important stuff. Everything went very smoothly.

Drove to Flagler Beach today just to meet Jim Deen and Allen Gray. It was quite a reunion— almost 20 years have elapsed since we all worked together for the SRD. But we keep in touch. You just never know.

Danny Kolhage, Mayor Pro Tem, 2014, Monroe County, Florida says . . .

Budd Post was the face of PBS&J. He devoted many years of service and countless hours to improving Florida and the Florida Keys. There was a time when PBS&J was subject to criticism from the commission. But Budd handled it as a true statesman and with great integrity. He was sophisticated. He was above getting down in the mud of political issues.

Budd was a man of great credibility. He had a presence about him that was professional in every regard. He treated people respectfully. He was easy to work with—not demanding. I enjoyed working with Budd very much. He leaves a powerful legacy to the Florida Keys.

Between 1960, when PBS&J was founded, and 2010, when it sold for $280 million to London-based Atkins, it grew from a Florida company, capitalized by four founders, for $500, to an to an employee-owned international conglomerate, with 3,500 employees, operating out of some 80 offices that billed nearly $800 million in a single year.

That didn't happen just because.

PBS&J followed a thought-through, expertly executed model. It was innovative. Proactive. Personal.

Key employees shared profits. That created an environment of ownership. That environment led to actions and decisions that were made by owners, not employees.

That was powerful.

Alex Jernigan says . . .

> *PBS&J was an exciting place to work. As we grew, we continued to expand our scope of services. Employees were appreciated. Inspired. Empowered. Invested. They were individuals, not numbers.*
>
> *PBS&J is a classic example of how to build a very successful organization. Anyone interested in doing the same should study its model. Then, build on it.*
>
> *It is my honor to present specifics of the PBS&J model:*
>
> ✓ *Keep your promises.*
> ✓ *Deliver on time, and within budget.*
> ✓ *Complete top-notch work and charge reasonable fees.*
> ✓ *Treat clients like family.*
> ✓ *Develop a personal relationship with clients and potential clients—pick up the telephone, talk face-to-face, go to lunch,*

send handwritten notes. Do NOT simply "shoot" an email or a text message.

✓ Avoid shortcuts.
✓ Build your reputation. Then, stand on it.
✓ Conduct yourself as a lady or gentleman.
✓ Develop and maintain trust.
✓ Hire excellent consultants who will support your business—for instance, a corporate attorney, CPA, computer technician.
✓ Surround yourself with people who display impeccable moral values—integrity, honesty, honor, decency.
✓ Perform to the very best of your ability—every day. Then, stretch. Go beyond your comfort zone.
✓ Hire employees who will perform "above and beyond." Then, compensate them accordingly.
✓ Reward people with intangibles. Say, "Thank you. . . . I appreciate you. . . . I respect you."
✓ When employees do not fit the organization, terminate them.
✓ Learn from your competition.
✓ Become active in local and national professional associations.
✓ Become active in local civic and political organizations.
✓ Give back to your community by volunteering.
✓ Love your work.

It's simple, but not easy.

Nonetheless, PBS&J did it.

And you can too.

Budd, himself, was a stellar example of staying active in professional, civic, and political organizations—of giving-back to his community.

He served on:

- ✓ Board of Florida Keys Community College
- ✓ Florida's School Board of Regents
- ✓ Board of the School of Engineering at Florida International University
- ✓ Board of Directors of the Florida Engineering Society
- ✓ American Society of Civil Engineers, Committee of Professional Practice
- ✓ National Society of Professional Engineers
- ✓ Society of American Engineers
- ✓ Fellow of the Florida Engineering Society (Engineer of the Year Award 1977)
- ✓ Florida State Board of Engineers and Land Surveyors
- ✓ Miami Chapter of the Florida Engineering Society, where he received the Engineer of the Year Award

Budd gave-back to his community as a member of:

- ✓ Greater Miami Chamber of Commerce
- ✓ Rotary
- ✓ Elder at the Miami Springs Presbyterian Church

PBS&J established the Howard M. Post Award for Technical Achievement, in Budd's honor.

And, above all, Howard Malvern Post—Budd, with *two* D's—loved his work.

Budd wrote in his diary . . .

> Picked up Dock Rogers at the office at 0530 to go to Key West to attend meeting of Engineering Contractors Examining Board. The meeting was dull and smoky, but necessary for me to be part of it all.
>
> Rotary today—Secretary's day, so took Jean.
>
> Off to Lauderdale at 6:00 to attend meeting of Society of Engineers—need to discuss union's latest activities. Home about midnight. Tired.
>
> Home at 5:30 tonite—first time in months I didn't have a meeting of some sort to attend in the evening.
>
> Was elected chairman of Board of Deacons tonight. It's going to be a tough year, with John Long already resigned and Stanway likely to quit because of a few troublemakers—and the ministers' votes against Barbara Yonteck at Presbytery.
>
> Some days I really, really can't believe how much I love what I do.

Each PBS&J project was different. Yet, each followed the same basic process.

Bob Harris says . . .

> *Let's take the Monroe County Road System as a project process example. You see, there was a local road system, state road system, and federal road system. The four hundred and seventy-six miles of local roads were under the jurisdiction of Monroe County. So, the Monroe County Commission authorized PBS&J to study those roads and recommend how they should spend the County's gas tax money to improve them.*
>
> *As the general consulting engineers, we drove the roads, took pictures, and determined which ones served the most people and which ones were in the worst condition. We learned the County's gas tax dollar cash flow. Then, we developed a formula and recommended how the County should prioritize its dollars to improve the most roads in the shortest period of time. That, in itself, was a very involved project.*
>
> *After the County Commission adopted PBS&J's recommendations, we were authorized to design the roads. Then, our in-house plans were put out to bid. Contractors bid on the projects. We recommended a contractor. The County awarded the contract. PBS&J, then, inspected the contractor's work to make sure it was completed according to our plans and specifications.*

So, the process for the Monroe County Road System project was typical for a road project, sewer project, water project—basically any project. In summary: PBS&J assessed the need, determined priorities, developed recommendations, presented recommendations, received approval, completed the design, solicited bids, and inspected the contractor's work.

But there's more: Florida has a law called The Consultant's Competitive Negotiations Act. *This law specifies that consulting engineering work is a professional service that is not put out to bid. That means that municipalities must select an engineering firm based on its qualifications— not its price.*

Admittedly, PBS&J didn't get every project, but we got most of what we went after. Why? We had a great reputation. And we lived up to it. Always.

Budd wrote in his diary . . .

Got the bad news from Monohan this morning that SRD is objecting to the Monroe County Master Plan Contract. He is kinda embarrassed and I wonder who is behind this. Monohan <u>knows</u> we would do the best job. Oh well. Next. Later today I met with Anderson, McCue, and Park and resolved the questions about our proposed contract to do NW 22 Ave. I trust it will proceed according to plan.

Over the course of 50 years, PBS&J worked for many clients and completed hundreds of projects.

For instance . . .

Keys projects:

- SR 905 (CR997) from Lake Surprise through Elliot's Key
- SR 905A (CR997A) Card Sound Road from Dade/ Monroe Line to Atlantic Ocean
- Card Sound Bridge, including four small bridges along SR905 Alignment
- Ocean Reef Club: Land development projects and design of Florida's first Reverse Osmosis Water Treatment Plant and Wastewater Plant
- City of North Key Largo Beach: Survey and Master Plan
- Duck Key (now Hawk's Cay) Land Development Project
- Plantation Key Government Center: Building and Site Design
- U.S. 1 Key Largo to Key West: Construction management for replacement of 37 bridges, including 7 Mile Long and Long Key
- Monroe County Secondary Road System: Planning and repairing prioritization for some 700 miles of roads
- Key West Harbor Redevelopment and Cruise Ship Docks

- Monroe County Key West Courthouse and Jail Additions
- Florida Keys Aqueduct Authority: Miscellaneous Pipeline and Well Field projects
- Rehabilitation of four Duck Key Bridges
- Port Bougainville
- Windley Key Quarry State Geological Site
- Monroe County Solid Waste System
- Layout of Hercules Missile Site 40 on North Key Largo for U.S. Corps of Engineers after Cuban Missile Crisis

Florida Projects:

- Palm Lakes Industrial Park—Hialeah
- Miami Lakes New Town Development
- City of Miami Springs General Consultant
- City of Miami Springs Wastewater System
- NW 22 Avenue Bascule Bridge Design over Miami River
- Aventura Land Development Projects
- Metrorail/Metro Mover Design
- North Miami Solid Waste Disposal Site
- North Miami 23 Million Gallons/Day Wastewater Treatment Plant
- Homestead Extension of Florida's Turnpike
- Villages of Homestead
- Downtown Homestead Krome Avenue Main Street Scape
- General Consultant for Florida's Turnpike

- Layout of U.S. Army Corps of Engineers Missile Defense System in Dade and Monroe Counties after Cuban Missile Crisis
- I75 in Lee and Manatee Counties
- Celebration Development at Disneyworld
- Disney World Miscellaneous Projects
- FEMA Flood Insurance Mapping: Florida and Nationwide
- FDOT Roadway and Bridge Projects Statewide
- Orlando Expressway Authority Toll System
- Miami-Dade Expressway Authority Toll System

United States Projects:

- FEMA Emergency Services Nationwide
- Atlanta Expressway Toll System
- Georgia DOT: Statewide Roadway and Bridge Projects
- Dallas-Ft. Worth Expressway and Interstate System
- Texas DOT Statewide Roadway and Bridge Projects
- Galveston, Texas Harbor Improvements
- Los Angeles Expressway and Interstate System
- California DOT Statewide Roadway and Bridge Projects
- Las Vegas Expressway and Casino Development Projects
- Nevada DOT Statewide Roadway and Bridge Projects
- U.S. Army Corps of Engineers at U.S. Military Bases Nationwide Planning and Redevelopment Projects

International projects:

- Jack Tar Hotel and Wastewater System: West End, Grand Bahama Island
- U.S. Steel Cement Plant Layout: Freeport, Grand Bahama
- U.S. Navy Anti-submarine Warfare Downrange Facilities: Andros Island, Bahamas
- Land development Project, Novosibirsk, Russia
- Central American Farm to Market Roadway System: Honduras
- Panama Canal Zone Projects for Jacksonville District U.S. Army Corps of Engineers:
  - Rocket Storage Revetment Area at Howard Air Force Base, Canal Zone
  - Howard Air Force Base Utility System Repairs
  - Site Surveys at Ft. Clayton, Ft. Albrook, and Coco Solo Naval Air Station
  - U.S. Army Ranger/U.S. Navy Seals Field Fortifications and Obstacle Siting and Design for the Jungle Warfare School at Ft. Gulick, Ft. Sherman, and Ft. Davis on the Atlantic side of the Isthmus
  - Surveying for Navy—Virgin Islands

Each project enhanced countless lives.

Budd wrote in his diary . . .

> George and I went to PWD to try to get a work order permitting us to go ahead with the design

of the 22 Avenue road project—the Commission approved our contract this morning!

Went to see Alan Stewart, Port Authority Director this afternoon—we're working on the airport!!!

Up to Jacksonville this morning and negotiated the contract with the Corps: $19, 469 to prepare plans and specs (in 6 weeks) for $387,000 worth of temporary improvements to the missile sites— mostly electric lights, mess halls, and shower facilities.

Negotiated contract with Navy for additional work at Boca Chica this morning—then flew to Jax with Bill Bradley and stopped at Jax Dist. office. Was advised that we had been selected for Panama job—about $1.5 million of construction at Howard AFB, Canal Zone!!

It's 1968 and we are sure bursting out the seams of our office space. Bob and I met with Ode Cox and Bob Chapman of the SRD to go over the North Dade Causeway project, which we will design. It will be a big job for us.

Up early and off to Ocean Reef in the rain. Met with Sibley at 0900 to discuss development of North Key Largo Beach and its relationship to Ocean Reef—of mutual interest. My ideas are the best:

1. Ultimately incorporation of O.R. as/into municipality
2. Solid waste disposal

3. Air strip
4. Range
5. Contractors equipment yards/
    headquarters.

They'll do it.

Visited US Department of Commerce office for foreign trade info. and stopped in for a minute at our DART office. Projects continue to expand. Grow.

Don't remember minor things today, but this was the day Liteco appeared before the Planning/ Zoning Board of Boynton Beach, seeking re-zoning of the Sandhill Project—700 acres. We had dinner at 5:30 in Del Ray and got set up for the presentation at 7:30. It took two hours, at which time it was unanimously approved!!! Got home at midnight.

Card Sound Bridge Groundbreaking, 1968

Jimmy says . . .

> *It's impossible to say exactly how many projects PBS&J completed. But of all of them, Card Sound Bridge was probably Dad's favorite.*
>
> *Dad loved the Florida Keys. He would do anything to make the Florida Keys a better place to live, work, and play. The Card Sound Bridge is only one of two ways motorists can leave or enter the Florida Keys (the other us U.S. 1). Before Dad got involved, the Card Sound Bridge was, literally, dead in the water.*
>
> *Dad was very, very proud of that bridge. My goal is to get it renamed "The Howard M. (Budd) Post Bridge." In the meantime, I call it, "Budd's Bridge."*

Back in 1921, people were just starting to discover southern Florida. So, the Miami Motor Club was eager to make fishing easily accessible—after all, great fishing would bring more tourists, and more tourists would bring more money. And folks with real estate interests were eager to gain easy access to thousands of acres of wilderness in the Upper Keys—after all, developing and selling land was their business.

So, Dade and Monroe County Commissioners agreed to build a highway connecting Florida City to Key Largo. And in 1922, Monroe County approved a $300,000 bridge bond issue—if, and only if, Dade County agreed to oversee constructing the 11 mile-long Card Sound Road, leading to the new drawbridge. Well, as commissioners do, they haggled back and forth, but eventually, sealed a deal.

Typical government, progress was slow, and complications nearly halted construction. Still, by late summer 1926, the road and bridge were almost finished. Then, in September 1926, the Great Miami Hurricane—a cat 4 storm—ripped through South Florida, destroying the road and the bridge.

Okay. Not so great. But engineers repaired the road and rebuilt the bridge to accommodate storm surge. In January 1928, the 2,800-foot, wooden Card Sound Bridge opened to traffic. But its troubles weren't over.

In 1944, a fire caused serious damage. Then, in 1947, another fire and another cat 4 hurricane made Monroe County officials throw up their hands. "Enough, already! The Card Sound Bridge is closed—for good."

Well, for the next 20 years, various schemes to increase access between the Keys and mainland Florida came and went to no avail.

Then, Budd Post stepped in. The Card Sound Bridge's woes were over.

Budd traced the Card Sound Bridge project in his diary . . .

> Lunch at Carriage Club with Harry Harris, Gerald Saunders. Then off to district office to meet with Monohan, Davidson, and (unexpectedly) Senator Spottswood. Usual road problem discussions,

plus interesting preliminary sparring re: financing and construction of Card Sound Bridge.

Went to Jax to Corps office with Pete Kelly, Tubby Field, Howard Riley, Jim Glass to argue the Card Sound Bridge permit. They surprised us! (Col. Tabb and McKnight). The Fla. Conversation Dept. had requested a 65 foot clearance—so they are holding that request. On to Tallahassee (we were traveling in Ocean Reef's Navajo) to lobby the cabinet for the dredging permit.

Attended cabinet meeting—Kirk in usual form—since we had agreed not to fight for 55 foot clearance everything else was OK.

Key West—and the commission authorized the advertisement bids for the Card Sound project!!

Lunch with Gene Bechamps at University Club prior to meeting with Tubby Field, McCreedy et. al. re. improvements to Old Card Sound Road, required to get traffic to our soon-to-be-constructed Card Sound Bridge. Wilbur Sith & Assoc. are not satisfied with resurfacing of existing road; are demanding more and we'll have to provide it—somehow!

Flew to Key West at 8:30 via Southeast—Commission meeting at 2:00PM—opened bids on Card Sound Project. Our estimate was $1.8 million.

At 2:00 the Card Sound Bridge cleared the first hurdle—the commission took bids on the bonds and received one—from Goodbody—and it was accepted!

The Commission finally selected Key West State Bans as trustee for Card Sound Bond funds.

Left office about 1000 with Jimmy—took one of Capelleti's pickups and some survey markers and headed for Keys via Card Sound project. Dredging still proceeding—test piles complete—beginning pier piles.

Off to Card Sound at 0800 to see what the problem was with the channel pier cofferdams; there was no problem; Hills just wasn't sure.

July 1, 1969! Red letter day. Card Sound Bridge was dedicated today—Jeanne, Matt, Sue, Jimmy, and Mom, and I attended—I introduced speakers etc. A great day—and probably the most significant day in my career—as far as history is concerned!

Bob Harris says . . .

We worked hard but we also knew how to have a great time.

Funny story . . . In late 1962, we got a job in Panama, so Budd, Buckley, and I went to the Panama Canal Zone on a recon trip to check out the bases where we were going to do the work.

One day, after we finished our business, we decided to ride the train to Cologne. So, there we were—me, Budd, and Buckley—walking around,

223

sightseeing, having a great time. Before long, we took a left turn onto Cash Street.

Unbeknown to us, Cash Street was where the prostitutes hung out. They were falling out windows, soliciting business. Buckley—"Mr. Stiff"—was appalled.

But Budd? Budd stopped and price-shopped up and down the street. He didn't buy, but he sure had fun looking!

Bob Harris, JOB, Cristobal-Colon CZ Oct 63

Bob Harris and John Buckley survey the streets of Panama

Budd's version of the story was slightly more staid.

Budd wrote in his diary . . .

Spent the day meeting various people concerned with our job and inspecting the site for the rocket storage facilities at Howard AFB in Panama.

Up at 0630 and off again to examine the site, locate personnel, estimate time required to do things, etc. Talked to Grand Foster of Foster-Williams Inc, who is a famous American ex-patriot; the IRS is after him, but I'm for him! Will probably rent a truck and dozer from them.

Had a conference at the Panama Canal Company Administrative Building, with Mr. Frank Lerchin, Chief Design Engr., and Bob Stewart, Chief Geologist. That Canal Co. is an experience! The epitome of Bureaucracy!

Had dinner at the de Tessepi Room of Panama Hilton ($15 for 3!) and then visited the casino for half an hour. It was my first experience in such a place, and I found it interesting. Bed at 1030.

Up at 0545 and after fast breakfast caught the 0710 train for Cologne. Enjoyed the train ride and the walk around the city. Back to Ancon on the 0950 train, arriving at 1115. After lunch checked out of the Tivoli and made our way to Tocumen Airport via the sightseeing route—with

"Church" as our driver.

Home aboard the Inter-Americano, arriving about 2200. Busy day at office tomorrow. Must catch up.

Alex Jernigan says . . .

Municipal engineers are not just engineers. They are good politicians. They take lots of

pressure—usually dirty pressure—from the press and sometimes politicians. PBS&J continually fought off that pressure. And we did it well.

Budd wrote in his diary . . .

Tallahassee on the early flight. Addressed the Governor (Kirk) and the Cabinet briefly, representing Monroe County re: Alabama Jack's lease. They refused to consider Monroe's claim for the money! Afterward, met with Tom Adams (Lt. Gov-Elect). Gave a PBSJ check for $10,000—an unrestricted gift to Florida Institute of Technology.

Had lunch today with Miami Mayor Dave Kennedy—re: future political alliance. He talks pretty good.

Alex Jernigan continues . . .

Take the Florida Turnpike—PBS&J was hired by the State to manage and engineer the Florida Turnpike. By then, the Turnpike had already been built, and the press and politicians were trying to remove tolls. Well, the tolls were starting to generate excess revenues, so PBS&J encouraged the State to keep the tolls and use the money to make improvements. It was the right thing to do. We did that a number of times.

Budd wrote in his diary . . .

C of C meeting this afternoon all about toll plan. The wheels have shifted from the Turnpike

Authority to a joint County SRO finance plan. I spoke against the majority—"I am impressed by what you say, but it happens to be a bunch of garbage."

Alex Jernigan continues . . .

The Orlando-Orange County Expressway Authority (OOCEA) is a classic example of political pressure. (PBS&J worked as their general consultants for over thirty years.) The press bombarded the public with the idea that tolls should be removed from the first expressway OOCEA built. PBS&J recognized that removing tolls would create the worst mess ever. Complete chaos.

So, again, PBS&J did the right thing, and convinced OOCEA to keep the tolls and use the revenue to build new roads. Orlando now has an efficient, effective expressway system that consists of the Bee Line Expressway, East West Expressway, the Western Beltway, the Green Way Expressway, and numerous interchanges throughout Orlando.

As a matter of fact, PBS&J designed the toll road pass, making it the most recognized firm in the United States for automatic toll collection design. So, not only was PBS&J politically astute and technically competent, we were very, very innovative.

So, there you have it. Now you know the story. Now you know PBS&J's mission/vision was not just fancy words, written on slick paper.

PBS&J was a living organization that can and will be a model for many.

Are you in?

11.

Waterside

Conservation. It's a loaded word—a continuum with more sharp points than a porcupine.

To purists, the environment is self-evidently priceless. Land is lush, pure, pristine. Human interference, in the form of development, destroys balance.

To extremists, the environment is a natural resource to be maneuvered in the name of progress. Developed land is *better* land, no matter what consequences befall the ecosystem.

Then there was Budd Post. Budd loved the environment. He appreciated nature. Nature as *nature* was as important as breathing. Still, Budd believed that development— *responsible* development—improved inhabits of all life forms that share planet earth.

Neither purists nor extremists *liked* Budd. They did, though, *respect* him.

Jimmy says . . .

After Dad retired full-time from PBS&J and started working as their consultant, conservation became his passion. Sure, there are fanatical conservationists—environmentalists—tree huggers—who scoffed at what Dad did, because he did it to develop public land and personal property.

But think about this: PBS&J, as a firm, was at the forefront of conservation—of repairing man's damage to the environment. PBS&J spearheaded using wetlands to scrub effluent spewing out of sewage treatment plants and return it to clear water.

Their first project was the Orlando Easterly Wetlands Reclamation Project, built in the late '80s. The City of Orlando received five awards for the project, including the PBS&J Project Excellence Award and the State of Florida Governor's Environmental Award.

Not only did the project improve water quality, it targeted vegetation, which, in turn, attracted wild life. As of today [2014] well over one hundred bird species have been observed on the site and ten species, including the Florida sandhill crane, little blue heron, and even the endangered wood stork use the site as part of their habitat. In addition, part of the project is a wilderness park, with nature trails and seasonal camping facilities.

But that's just one example of what PBS&J and Dad designed to mitigate environmental damage. They were on the forefront of so many breakthroughs. Dad loved his Keys and would do whatever to preserve them—better them.

I'm confident Dad's love of nature started way back when he was a Boy Scout and continued throughout his life.

Budd wrote in his diary . . .

1940

Good morning—up about 7:00 am or so. Fed Moon (a horse) and then breakfast. The horses came during rest hours. Boy are they <u>horses!</u> <u>Love 'em.</u> Tried to catch Glenn and King. Had to saddle Moon and Duke to chase those devils all over the mountain. Boy, were they wild!

1945

Good Morning—quite a memorable day in the Army! Reveille and chow, and at 8:00 am, coming out of the Mess Hall there was beautiful, red sunrise. BUT, in the west, there was a complete, brilliant rainbow! Maybe that's a good omen.

1950

Another great day! Saw white-crowned pigeons today for the first time in my life. Ocean like glass, no breeze, no clouds. Left Snake Creek about 9:00 AM and off to the reefs. Hen and Chickens was absolutely beautiful, even to the green moray who inhabited the rocks immediately beneath our boat. All told we caught one barracuda, five yellowtails and assorted grunts. Finally got home about 7:00 pm . . . and tired!

1960

PV picked me up at 0700 and we went to Jean Crook's ranch. We were there ostensibly to serve as guides to any church people who might respond to an invitation to look at the site of the proposed Presbytery Camp Ground which Jean has offered as a gift. We had one such group, and the rest of the time we just enjoyed the scenery, including a wild hog, a deer, and a rat snake (in a hollow limb).

I'm in Panama on a job—this was my first encounter with tropical jungle at first hand, except for riding through mangrove swamps in Colombia. The size of the trees was amazing, as was the complete lack of insects, including mosquitoes.

1970

Went fishing with Capt. Gene Lowe out of Tavernier on the Katherine II, small snapper are already around the boulder breakwater. WOW!!!

After breakfast with Harry, Fred, and Chuck Little, packed up and left for home at 0830, dropping Fred in Perrine to pick up his jeep. On the way, passing through Crocodile Lake, saw about 10 spoonbills along with approximately same number of <u>white</u> pelicans. Beautiful!

Golf or fishing, always a great time

1980

Up early and off to Key West at 0630. Visited
No Name Key and while parked at the Old Ferry
landing, watching bird etc, saw two key deer—
first time ever in the wild. Two does, about the
size of a small police dog.

Up at 0530 and left for Fort Myers at 6:20 am via
Alligator Alley and I-75. It was a beautiful (and
nostalgic) trip across the Everglades. Saw a doe
alongside of the road in the Big Cypress areas,
and there are a gillion signs of panthers crossing.

Rita and Carl Edwards came by as scheduled
around 11:00 am and we had lunch and showed
them around Ocean Reef until their departure
about 6:00 pm. It was nice to see them—after all,
Rita was responsible for introducing Jeanne to
me. But the highlight of the day (for me) was the
pair of yell-crowned night herons (plus a juvenile)

that waded the flats just south of the house. The flats were dry because of a -0.8 low tide (lowest for '87) and the birds were gorgeous. It took me quite a while to identify them—they were a long way from their customary ranges.

1990

Beautiful full moon tonite—came up out of the ocean. **WOW!** God, I love this place [Waterside].

Big tree clean up from Hurricane Andrew today. Still never too busy to fish (caught 5 little fish) and fed Herman (my "very own" white crane).

After breakfast, I saw a strange sight—four porpoises were on the flats north of the house, cruising around in three feet of water! Two of them swam up to within 25 feet of the mangroves and swam north in the little natural channel along the mangroves! At sight of the first fin, I thought it was a big shark!

About 11:00 am while cleaning the car, found a half-grown buzzard that showed up in the carport, on foot. His wings were black, but the rest of him was white down. Called Sandy Sprint (local wildlife expert) and he said to turn him loose by some bushes, and the parents will probably find him and feed him, which is what I did. He reacted with more strength than I thought he had from first appearances; he may make it if the mosquitoes or coons don't get him first!

It was a beautiful day, warm, sunny, etc, so the water was not too cold to stand in at <u>low tide.</u> Last night was a rather spectacular astronomic event: two planets were in very close proximity to the moon, and through the field glasses, I could see the outline of the whole moon, although most of it was in the shadows. The first view I had was about 3:00 am +/-, the second view was at sunrise and the planets were still visible, in different positions of course, and the largest one was just above the "point" of the moon, but even with the field glasses only the portion of the moon receiving the sun's rays was visible.

During the '70s and '80s, Budd perpetuated—memorialized—his respect for the environment by devoting his time and talents to "Saving Paradise."

Senator Bob Graham says . . .

> *When I was in the legislature, I was instrumental in passing legislation that was entitled* Saving Paradise: The Florida Environmental Land and Water Management Act of 1972. *Among other things it called for designating areas of Florida that were under uniquely severe growth pressure to have State oversight.*

> *One of the first areas of critical concern was the Florida Keys, which eventually led to a number of more focused planning efforts, one of which was Key Largo. PBS&J and Budd, himself, were heavily involved in those efforts.*

On September 5, 1984, Budd wrote in his diary . . .

> Was appointed by Gov. Graham to the committee
> to develop a habitat preservation plan for Upper
> Key Largo.

The *North Key Largo Habitat Conservation Plan* was prepared to help implement the 1972 *Florida Environmental Land and Water Management Act*. It focused, especially, on land around Crocodile Lake National Wildlife Refuge—land the U.S. Fish and Wildlife Services Agency designated to protect a critical breeding and nesting habitat for the threatened American crocodile and other wildlife, including the Key Largo wood rat.

Budd's committee worked long and hard to complete the plan. As the 11th hour approached, the *Florida Keys Keynoter* reported:

Time Is Running Out For Conservation Plan

By Phil Foley

Upper Keys News Director

15 June 1986: KEY LARGO—The clock is ticking ever louder for the North Key Largo Habitat Conservation Plan (HCP) Committee.

The HCP drafting committee held its last meeting June 12 and the full committee has only two more meetings scheduled before the gubernatorial order creating it expires July 30.

"I for one," said Charles Siemon, the group's consulting attorney, "am not anxious to see this extended for one minute."

Jim Murley assured the group the state Department of Community Affairs, "will not ask for an extension of the committee."

The panel, which represents landowners on North Key Largo, environmentalists and government officials, has until July 30 to develop a plan for the future development of land oceanside off State Road 905 between Ocean Reef Club and Port Bougainville.

Most of the land bayside of the road has been purchased or is slated for purchase for the Crocodile Lake National Wildlife Refuge.

Budd Post, who owns land in the area, urged the committee to exclude six platted subdivisions from the HCP.

The six, he said, "have no biological importance (to the endangered species in the area), have cleared land, and people living there."

Mr. Post said not excluding Knowleson Colony, Gulfstream Shores, Ocean Reef Shores, JHT, Nichols and Madera Village would be "asking for $100 worth of trouble for five cents worth of benefit." No decision on the subdivisions was reached.

If the Monroe County Commission approves the HCP for inclusion in the County's land-use plan, it would place a moratorium on development in the North Key Largo area until Aug. 1, 1988, to give the government time to purchase land in the area.

Douglas Halsey, a Miami attorney representing one of the landowners, said that unless the state is planning on purchasing all the land in the six subdivisions, there is "no reason to include them in the moratorium."

Mr. Halsey's client, Eddie Gong, is already proceeding with plans to build a project on his land adjacent to Ocean Reef Club. It is unclear what effect the moratorium would have on these plans.

Even with County approval for the project, Mr. Gong would still need a section 10 permit from the U.S. Fish and Wildlife Service. A Section 10 permit allows for the incidental taking of endangered species during a construction project.

Mr. Post, who has scrapped plans for condominiums in favor of single-family homes on his property, is pursuing a Section 10 permit independently of the HCP process.

Frank Gardner, another North Key Largo property owner, noted that including the wildlife refuge, less than 10 percent of North Key Largo will ever be developed under the HCP.

William Westray, a Key West political activist, urged that anyone purchasing land in the area in the future be warned of endangered species.

The full HCP committee is slated to meet June 19 in the community room of the Key Largo Library. The group's final meeting is slated for July 30.

Eventually, the *North Key Largo Habitat Conservation Plan* was completed and went on to serve as a model for the *Key Largo Community Master Plan*. Monroe County staff used portions of the *Master Plan* to guide land development activities in and around Key Largo.

This plan is part of a community-driven planning process that addresses the individual needs of the island communities in the Florida Keys. The *Key Largo Livable Community Keys Plan* covers the area between Mile Markers 97 and 107, excluding the offshore islands. The Key Largo local comprehensive planning process (LCP), which started in May 2004, engaged the community to determine important island features, identified issues affecting these conditions, and related desires of the community to future development activities.

Why did Budd have such a strong interest in the *North Key Largo Habitat Conservation Plan* and in the Key Largo LCP process? Short answer: Elbow Light Club and Waterside.

It all started in 1968, when Budd bought ten acres in North Key Largo, directly on the Atlantic Ocean.

Budd wrote in his diary . . .

> March 29, 1968: Received $2000 from PBMS Inc. as part payment on $7,000 note. I made the first mortgage payment on the Keys Lands: $2270. Mom paid half.

Jimmy says . . .

> *Dad loved Key Largo. He was very involved in its development. But his primary focus was his dream home—Waterside—and his plan for a developed Elbow Light Club. This was more than just his focus. It was his passion. Purpose. Probably obsession. And Dad moved heaven and earth to make it happen.*

Bob Harris says . . .

Budd knew everybody who took leading roles in developing North Key Largo. PBS&J did engineering for many of them. Through the grapevine, Budd heard that a parcel of land (about ten acres) off State Road 905, between Ocean Reef Club and Port Bougainville was available. So, he decided to buy it.

During the '70s, Budd visited his Key Largo property regularly. He cleared vegetation. He built a dock. He started planning the first of several development options for the property. He started construction of the first house on the site—a house he called the *Gate House, Key Largo Property One,* or, simply, *KLP #1.*

Budd traced the process/progress in his diary . . .

May 29, 1970: Clear in Key Largo. Main project was to police up all the trash. Took it to Ted Carter's dump. Also installed padlock on the newly constructed chain link gate.

January 23, 1971: Worked on property until noon, cleaning and burning and measuring for dock.

April 20, 1977: Got building permit for the dock slab and then talked to Lt. Landa (no Lt. in charge) at Plantation substation about the Key Largo property. He says "Post it and we will catch the garbage dumpers."

May 1, 1978: Picked up four different sketches prepared by Barden for Key Largo. Must decide which one to use in establishing location of Gate House. We'll move on as planned from there.

During the '80s, Budd did "move on" with his plan to develop Elbow Light Club. At the same time, Monroe County (in response to the State of Florida designating the Florida Keys as "an area of unique concern") revised its comprehensive plan and land development regulations. Restrictions—*lots* of restrictions—were imposed.

Well, Budd was a consummate politician without being a *politician*. He got it. So, instead of pursuing the impossible, he revised his original plan for Elbow Light Club and plotted his land into sites for eleven single family homes, each with ocean access, via an existing water basin.

Budd went "all out" to enact his revised plan, with Waterside (Budd's dream home) being first on his list.

Bob Harris says . . .

> *Budd, Jimmy, my son John, and I surveyed Budd's land, and Budd made plans to develop it into townhouses and condominiums and call it "The Elbow Light Club." But it didn't all work out as Budd hoped it would.*
>
> *When he started to develop it according to the plat plan that had been approved by the County Commission and recorded in the County's offices, the extreme environmentalists stopped him cold.*

So, as a trade-off Budd settled for building the dream house he called Waterside and one other smaller house.

Budd was smart. He negotiated the deal to preserve perpetual access rights for his family.

Budd wrote in his diary . . .

September 11, 1980: Up and off to County Commission meeting at Plantation sub-courthouse. All the commissioners indicate that I would have 'no problem' with item 6-G on the agenda—the Key Largo Basin Permit. They finally got to it at 3:00 pm.

July 30, 1981: When we got to Bill's condo [Coral Harbor], he handed me the [US Army] Corps [of Engineers] permit for the basin—at last! It took us about two and a half years to get the three permits required—County, State and Federal!

October 30, 1981: Got building permit for the basin today and I am going to start construction immediately to forestall even the remotest possibility of it being stalled by a 'moratorium' or other catastrophe.

April 19, 1982: Went to Mr. Plato Cox at Auto Marine Engineers. I asked him if he could help me find a mast for the top of the Island Home [soon to be called just Waterside]. He said he had one in the yard. It came off the Coast Guard Cutter Nemesis, according to him. The cutter sank a Nazi submarine in WWII.

242

January 19, 1983: Jeanne and I agreed that we would go all out this year to (1) build the Island House (Waterside), borrowing the necessary construction funds and (2) secure final approval on a MPD [major development plan] with as many units as possible.

March 21, 1983: Big event of the day—signed contract with builder to complete the Island House (Waterside)!

May 1984: Clean up on Waterside just about finished. Jim came down this morning and helped start the moving into Waterside. Moved the plan file from the downstairs office in KLH to my new office in Waterside—and that was quite a little project in itself.

Jeanne says . . .

Even though Budd wasn't allowed to develop the land the way he wanted to he was allowed to build Waterside. And Budd truly, truly loved Waterside.

Sure, Budd was an engineer himself but he still had the architect work with a structural engineer, because he wanted Waterside built like a bridge, so it could never be damaged in a hurricane. Budd's dream was to hunker down in Waterside during a major hurricane and laugh at the storm.

Budd wrote in his diary . . .

August 23, 1992: It is now 10:00 PM, and I have been going like a bomb (to quote Alan Gray) since 0600—getting WS ready for Hurricane Andrew. We secured 871 Lake Drive pretty quickly, gave key to Barnes next door and left about 1000. Called Monroe Sheriff's Dept. and they said residents could get thru the road block at Fla. City—and it was very easy. Traffic north bound (evacuating Keys was bumper to bumper (almost). Jew Fish Creek Bridge was locked down; stopped at Winn Dixie for a few supplies (not very crowded); and arrived at WS about 1100. Spent a long nine hours from then on—three trailers and two boats and one car to be parked in protected spots up in hammock and/or by Harlee's house. [Almost forgot—he called for advice on shutters—and we found the pins were missing for the porch panels—so he improvised.] I had to install the shutters over the roof gable ends, all of which took most of an hour. Secured the dock shack (sorta), hauled lose lumber away from beach, took dock ladder off and stowed it in shop, put things in shop up on benches where possible, shut off water and power to Harlee's . . . Supper about 8:30, and now I'm about to turn in, everything boarded up that can be—but I expect some leakage—probably around some exterior doors, depending on wind direction. As of now, center is expected at Miami about dawn tomorrow—a Class IV storm. [Electric generator seems to be ready for full duty; lets hope we don't need it!] Wind has not yet started to blow—but direction (N) is consistent with broadcast locations of eye. Later: Power went off about 2:00 AM (Jeanne was awake off and on) but I slept until about 0600.

August 24, 1992: We were really fortunate!! The eye of the storm passed north of us, so strongest winds were from the west, which kept wave action down, dampened the storm surge, and kept us in the lee of Key Largo in general. As a result, we had no structural or water damage of any kind to speak of, and when I walked out to 905 around 1000, the worst problem was several fallen tree limbs. According to the radio, the south half of Dade County took a terrible blow. Cranked up the generator again this morning, and it would not start; finally figured it must be the battery that I used last night—got one out of the boat, and the generator has now been running for about 10 hours—and it will have to keep running (mainly for refrigeration) because when we made a run to Ocean Reef and Downtown Card Sound this afternoon, we could see downed wire all along Card Sound Road and including the aerial crossing at Card Sound; crews from FKEC were hard at work, but I would guess it may take several days. Downtown Card Sound is almost totally destroyed—just a mass of wreckage with Alabama Jack's the only one looking to be salvageable. The awning cover over the Toll Booth served as a beautiful sail—and pulled the whole supporting structure up by the roots and it is lying in the canal on its side! Went to Ocean Reef gatehouse and Chuck Broeman was there (with 2 FHP cars and 2 Monroe Sheriff Dept. cars and deputies) to ensure that no unwanted visitors got in; we didn't even try. Chuck says they did have damage. Tried many times today to get a call thru to Jim—but to no avail. He must have been right in the center of the eye—and there were many casualties. We think they must be alright, or we would have heard; we are praying, and will go up in the morning by car, if we can get there.

August 25, 1992: What a birthday! Up at 0630 and made ready to go north to see what happened to Jim & family, the homestead on 871, etc. Left for Jim's by way of US1, of course. Card Sound Rd. being closed. The traffic north was light until we got to about Cutler Ridge, although southbound was heavy, mostly Monroe County evacuees returning. We stayed on US1 and the first damage noted was the FPL transmissions line: almost every pair of poles was snapped off all the way from the county line north. The "damage curve" escalated sharply when we approached Florida City, and it and Homestead were shocking— looked like aftermath of atomic attack. PBSJ office mostly intact—but many glass windows out, affording direct entry. Thence to Jim's house via US 1, west on 112 St. to Balloway and west on SW 108. He and whole family are okay, although house suffered some minor structural damage— large broken windows in living room, plus a lot of limbs down. Power and telephone out, and water is temporarily not potable. After counting noses and exchanging information we left for M.S. via Palmetto (no problems) and got to 871 Lake Drive straightway. More good news: no damage to house or garage at all, and 5 minutes after we walked in, power came on! So we have lights, AC, refrigeration, TV, and a little telephone. The neighborhood is a mess of downed trees (as is all of MS) but damage doesn't appear to be as severe further south. We left to come back, this time, by Turnpike, and that was a small mistake: Took us 1 hour and 15 minutes to get off the Turnpike and thru the check point at "Last Chance Saloon." Checked in at house (generator still functions fine although it has used half of a full tank of gas!). Made a run to O.R. to get rid of accumulated garbage in the drums on Card Sound Rd. and drove around and checked out the damage, which was noticeably more severe than at our house. Home, TV dinners, and to bed.

Important: At Waterside, our damage was confined to loss of trees and branches in the hammock and damage to the landscaping. However all of our strongest winds came from the west (because we were south of the eye). The proof, though, lies in the fact that our dock (which is not anchored down at the inboard side) never moved an inch. All this, and yet Pete Perdue's boat storage hangers at OR were heavily damaged as was other property around us. Waterside held true!!!

Jimmy says . . .

Regardless of the outcome of Elbow Light Club as Dad originally envisioned it, he loved Waterside. It was his special place in the world. For the next eight or nine years after he finished the house, he went back and forth between it and Miami Springs. But he spent the majority of his time at Waterside, doing consulting for PBS&J or working on his environmental projects. He enjoyed the heck out of that time in his life. He really did.

Budd wrote in his diary . . .

Spent all day in Waterside by myself, and it was great! A very stormy day with high winds and rain, but it was exciting. Like being on the bridge of a ship in a storm! And it's mine, all mine!!!

The dream come true

Jimmy continues . . .

I have so many wonderful memories of Waterside. Interesting story about when Dad and Mom first moved in . . . Dad was an excellent marksman. He had a Colt forty-five pistol and an M1 carbine from Korea. I remember going with him to the marina in Miami Beach, when he handed those guns over to Manuel Ray, as he was boarding the boat, heading out to raid Cuba. Well, along the way, Ray was stopped by the Bahamian Coast Guard, the guns were confiscated, and Dad never got them back. Too bad, because they were classic collectors' items.

Anyway, Dad never bought another gun. I bought him a twelve gauge shotgun and a Lugar May fourteen rifle when he and Mom moved into Waterside. Occasionally, he'd have a little fun shooting at clay pigeons. But the main reason I bought Dad the guns was for protection. I said, "No way are you moving into that house without a gun—just no way!"

Back in the seventies and eighties, the area around Waterside was totally isolated. AND it was like the Wild-Wild West. Before Waterside was built, smugglers showed up every night with boatloads of pot from Colombia and made their drop on Waterside's property. It was the biggest drug smuggling spot in South Florida.

After Mom and Dad moved in, guys from a law enforcement agency (back then, local sheriffs, Feds, Coast Guard, Marine Patrol, U.S. Customs, and DEA rotated watches at different locations along the coast) sat on the porch every night, with their big infrared binoculars, watching for drug smugglers. (This was before coastal radar.)

To this day [2014] the biggest pot bust in Florida's history happened right on Waterside's property. Around seventy-eight or seventy-nine, smugglers beached two thirty-five-foot cabin cruisers and a thirty-six-foot cigarette boat and left behind thirty-five tons of pot. Lucky, Dad never had an occasion to use his guns, but you'd better believe he needed them, just in case. And if push had ever come to shove, would he have used them? Heck, yeah!

Funny story: Dad was, for the most part, Mr. Proper. Well, one day he was at Waterside alone. He stepped out on the porch and the door closed behind him. He was locked out. Not only was he locked out, he was buck-ass naked. Well, back then, we kept the only hide-key clear out by the front gate. So, Dad didn't have any choice but to jump off the porch and hike, naked and barefoot, about a half-mile down what was then a rock road to get the key.

He probably trotted back because of the mosquitos. There were so many mosquitos that if you killed one, ten more buzzed up to its funeral.

But, then again, maybe Dad didn't trot back. It was the weirdest thing—mosquitos would swarm and bite the hell out of everyone, except Dad. I never did figure that one out!

Waterside was finished. Budd was content, but not complacent. It was time to build the remaining single family homes on the Elbow Light Club property. His first task was to obtain permits from county, state, and federal agencies.

The Key Largo wood rat, a federally designated endangered species, emerged as a major player. On some level, the Key

Largo wood rat, literally, held the "keys" to Elbow Light Club's ultimate development.

Budd's pet, Herman

Jeanne says…

>*Budd loved to fish. And he fished a lot. He also loved birds. Budd put up a pole behind our Waterside house so we could see Osprey nests and watch mama birds feed their babies.*

>*Then there was Herman. Herman was a white crane. At low tide, Herman would sit on the*

point. Budd would whistle, wade out, and throw fish. Well, Herman got so friendly, as soon as he heard Budd's whistle, he would fly down and follow Budd everywhere.

I must tell you that Budd was interested in conservation for his entire life. But if you had listened to the State you would have thought he was a criminal, determined to slay every wood rat on the planet.

Was Budd Post *really* the villain? Did the small, furry rodent, with cinnamon fur and bulging black eyes *really* succumb to the "heartless developer"?

Well, according to the April 24, 2014, *Tampa Bay Times*, Federal officials decided they could save the Key Largo wood rat from extinction. So, the government spent $12,000 a year, for almost 30 years, to breed wood rats and turn them loose in the wild. Even Disney's Animal Kingdom—the granddaddy of rat breeders—got involved.

The problem was after the wood rats were released into their natural habitat, feral cats (NOT Budd Post) wiped them out. So, the wildlife agency tried something different. Rats were turned loose on Palo Alto Key. (Feral cats don't live on Palo Alto Key.) This time, owls (NOT Budd Post) swooped down, and gobbled them up.

But the tax payers $360,000 was not spent in vain . . . A biologist followed a Key Largo wood rat's radio-tracking device. He stopped short. But, then, anyone who comes face-to-teeth with a 12 foot, carnivorous Burmese python (one of the world's five largest snakes) would probably do the same. Although big, invasive snakes are common in the Everglades, this was the first python spotted in the Keys. The biologist concluded, "Apparently, pythons can swim."

By the way, in case you're wondering: the snake swallowed both the rat and its radio-tracking device.

Anyway, Bob Harris says…

The tree huggers fought Budd tooth and nail. They actually tried to shut him down. You see, hardwood hammocks and elements of tropical forest habitats on Key Largo support five federally listed endangered species: American crocodile, eastern indigo snake, Key Largo cotton mouse, Schaus swallowtail butterfly, and Key Largo wood rat. Budd's primary problem was the wood rat.

Budd dealt with the powers that be by actually saving the wood rat. He moved it off his property to a location that made its life better. Still, Budd wasn't able to develop his property as he had intended.

Jimmy says . . .

I'll start at the beginning . . . Dad bought the property back in 1960. It was ten acres of upland and two underwater acres. (Back then, you could buy submerged land.) So, after Dad owned the land, he got a permit to dig a channel.

He had a devil of a time but that didn't stop Budd Post. He was the last person, ever, to receive a permit to dig a deep-water channel anywhere in the Keys.

So, after Dad got the permit to dig the channel, he went back to the State and said, "I'll make you a deal. I'll give you the eastern most underwater acre for free if you let me build a small island and break wall." The bureaucrats agreed. So, Dad hired contractors to dynamite through the coral and build the island, where Waterside sits.

Then, during the early nineties, Dad applied for a permit to dig the turning basin at the end of the channel, in the paved road through the woods. It was a total of an acre and a half that had to be cleared between the turning basin and the road.

When he first approached the Florida Department of Environmental Protection, they laughed at him and basically said, "No way! The Key Largo wood rat lives there. The wood rat is an endangered species. You can't mess with the wood rat." Well, "No way," was the wrong thing to say to Budd Post. The minute Dad heard "No way," he was even more determined to do what HE wanted to do.

Still, Dad always did whatever he did (either personally or through PBS&J) legally. He believed property owners have rights—but only if they follow the letter of the law. With that said, Dad would never do ANYTHING without a proper permit. One developer dug a series *of canals adjacent to Dad's property without permits. The State plugged them. Another developer dug two canals and built a big house off State Road 905. The State seized everything. Dad knew the legal consequences. In addition, he had personal ethical standards.*

Anyway, Dad decided he would relocate the wood rat. But before he did, he knew he needed a permit. Well, no one on the planet had ever relocated an endangered species. The officials didn't even have application forms. But that didn't stop Budd Post. It took him seven years, countless hours, and thousands of dollars of his own money to cut through the red tape of thirty-five government agencies. (By the way, Dad wasn't a wealthy man—he was land rich, cash poor, and damned determined.)

Budd wrote in his diary . . .

September 18, 1984: I left for Key Largo to meet Fish and Game representatives to review the wood rats on the property. Tim Regan from Tallahassee, plus Bob Smithe (Monroe biologist) plus Barbara (another wildlife scientist) counted nests.

November 21, 1984: Bill Roberts called about 2:00 pm having just come from a meeting with DCA. The proposed solution is this—they will not appeal if I will sign an agreement granting them status to 'approve' any permit arrangements that I make with FWS or GFC with respect to endangered species. Told Bill to go ahead, he will prepare the document and I will sign next week.

November 30, 1984: Called Bill Roberts office at 5:00 pm, De Grove [from DCA] signed the settlement agreement and we got by with an appeal by DCA!

April 17, 1985: Karen Achors came by at 1:30 pm and we talked about her ideas for wood rat preservation. Essentially it was this: forget the handful of animals involved (wood rats and cotton mice because their destruction would have no appreciable impact on the survival of the species.) Instead, offer to FWS and GFC to 'replace' the one acre of habitat to be destroyed, because the loss of the habitat is of some significance to the long term survival of the animals. She has some idea for cleaning up some trash dumps, fencing, and re-vegetation activities that would possibly be very acceptable to the various agencies. Sounds good and I will pursue it further with her.

April 29, 1985: Went to Karen Achors house to discuss her proposed approach to 'hammock enhancement' as a means of getting permits for incidental taking of the wood rats. She suggested some sites, and I will look at them. Started late this afternoon as matter of fact, looking at the ocean end of Ocean-Bay Road, where there is a significant stand of Schaus butterflies!

Jimmy continues...

Finally, the i's were dotted and the t's were crossed. Dad had his permit. As an aside, as soon as word got out, Dad got calls from every astonished developer between Florida and California asking, "How in the world did you pull THAT off!?" Dad deadpanned, "I'm a consultant. Send me a check, and I'll tell you."

Anyway, with his permit in hand, Dad was ready to conquer the wood rat. Well, during the Cuban Missile Crisis, the army built Nike missile sites up and down Florida's coast. They were the last line of defense against Soviet bombers. By the nineties, they had been decommissioned. One of the former sites was on Key Largo. So, Dad paid a contractor to bulldoze up the old asphalt road and a landscaper to plant indigenous trees and vegetation.

Then, Dad hired a team of scientists. (By the way, Dad used his money to pay for everything.) You see, wood rats build mound nests above ground. So Dad's scientists collected appropriate sticks and twigs, and laid them out on the site, ready for the wood rats. The wood rats didn't even have to forage through the woods to find materials for their nests.

The scientists then trapped the wood rats, measured them, tagged them, and transported them to the site. It was all on the up and up—a very lengthy and expensive process that ended up making wood rats' lives easier—better.

All along, the Feds and the Department of Environmental Protection inspectors watched to make sure wood rats didn't return to Dad's property. They didn't.

Budd wrote in his diary . . .

October 14, 1986: FWS wood rat permit day!

October 31, 1986: Wood rat day at Waterside! Getting ready for land clearing and wood rat research project!

July 8, 1987: We left Miami Springs at 0800 and checked the missile site. The water truck didn't show up yesterday, so Tom went to Matecumbe and borrowed Sankpells' water tank (200 gallons) from Mrs. Sherd. Weather is not cooperating—hot, over 90 degrees and not a drop of rain. Planting complete today. Julie Hovis apparently did not make the inspection visit that she planned for yesterday (or was it today)? Anyway we didn't see her.

Jeanne says . . .

Budd jumped through lots of hoops and spent lots of our money, but he finally relocated the wood rat. Then, he testified before Congress. He was actually the first person to ever speak in front of a congressional committee about relocating an endangered species. And Budd came out smelling like a rose. Congressmen were so impressed they ended up praising Budd for what he did for that pain in the butt rat!

Finally. The Key Largo wood rats enjoyed a new—better—home. Budd's two houses—Waterside and KLH #1—were finished. It was time to sell the remaining lots on Elbow Light Club's property to owners who would build their own single- family homes.

But wait . . . Budd needed approvals from Monroe County and state agencies.

By this time, Florida's new and tougher building standards for the Upper Keys were in place. And Budd was *Budd*—prudent. Pragmatic, Practical. After months of offers and counter offers, he sold Elbow Light Club's remaining platted lots to the State of Florida.

Budd wrote in his diary . . .

> January 30, 1990: Met Bill Roberts, Lonzo Cothron, Bob Beck [DNR surveyor] at 11:30 am to study on the ground Beck's contention that his study of aerial photos indicates that Lonzo had filled about four acres that were below mean high water (12 years ago!) and with permits and therefore the State should not buy back what they had originally owned. There is no doubt that he is technically correct, that land below the mean high water line was filled, but it is literally impossible to establish where the line was with any reasonable degree of precision, reasonable enough to call a property boundary. The purpose of DNR is to buy the land for conservation, not to find excuses to obstruct the sale.

March 8, 1990: Bill and I went to DNR for our 2:30 pm appointment with Butch Horn to discuss their written offer. The results were inconclusive. He made several statements about the limitations on the funding, how it might run out, etc. I was surprised to find that they apparently really want KLH#1, but Bill thinks they will give up, as part of their next offer, which is also supposed to be structured so as to let me retain lots 1 and 2. We'll see...and probably not as quickly as he promised, which was later next week.

October 22, 1990: Spent morning working over Bill Robert's first draft of our counter proposal to DNR.

November 15, 1990: Jack Harllee and I caught US Air at 0710 and went to Tallahassee. Argued and negotiated with Fred Saxon of DNR for two hours and finally agreed on the price (which was easy) $650,000, gave up $2,000 from our counter offer. But the discussion over where Jack could have the boat/davits/access were futile. It ain't over yet!

December 31, 1999: Went to Homestead to review fax from Owen Goodwyne and accepted it as written, trust DNR will have no further 'improvements' or what ifs.

March 26, 1991: At lunch time Bill Roberts called and said the Florida Cabinet passed (approved) the purchase of the property ($650,000) with little comment.

Budd's interest in Florida's Upper Keys extended beyond wood rats, Waterside, and the Elbow Light Club.

Bob Harris says . . .

> *John Pennekamp, founder of John Pennekamp Coral Reef State Park, was Budd's good friend. Back in the park's formative days, Budd was very involved in convincing the State of Florida to take it on as a park.*

The year was 1948. Movie aficionados sat in a darkened theatre. A black and white picture of a small boat, pitching on the high seas filled the big screen. The camera panned to a handsome man. He was sending a distress signal.

The man spoke into a ship-to-shore-phone. "My name is Frank McCloud. I'm about twelve miles off Boot Key Harbor . . . *Over.*"

A voice responded. "Hold your course. You're headed straight for Key Largo . . . *Key Largo!*"

Text scrolled across the screen . . . *"At the southernmost point of the United States are the Florida Keys, a string of small islands, held together by a concrete causeway. Largest of these remote coral islands is Key Largo."*

Almost overnight, Bogie and Bacall fans from around the nation flocked to what was once a sleepy, slow, well-kept secret . . . *Key Largo!*

By the late '50s, tourists had violated Key Largo's coral reef—the only living coral formation in the continental United States. Corals, seashells, sponges, and sea horses were hammered, chiseled, even dynamited from their rightful homes, all in the name of "souvenirs." By 1957, a handful of South Florida preservationists and prominent scientists had banned with the Marine Institute of Miami to designate a protected preserve.

Among them was an associate editor and columnist from the *Miami Herald*. His name was John D. Pennekamp. Mr. Pennekamp's credentials were impressive: he was instrumental in establishing Florida's Everglades National Park; he served as the first chairman of the Florida Board of Parks and Historic Memorials; he consulted with the U.S. Fish and Wild Life Service.

The group's efforts led the Florida Board of Parks and Historic Memorials to designate approximately 70 nautical square miles of the Florida Keys' reef track to become a permanent preserve and the first underwater park in the United States. In early 1960, President Dwight D. Eisenhower named it Key Largo Coral Reef Preserve.

But that name didn't ring true with Floridians. On December 10, 1960, Florida's Governor Thomas LeRoy Collins renamed the park John Pennekamp Coral Reef State Park.

It was, after all, the culmination of John Pennekamp's vision to preserve Key Largo's native birds, marine life, vegetation, coral reef, mangrove swamps, and tropical hammocks as they were formed, and as they should remain formed, forever.

Still, John Pennekamp Coral Reef State Park didn't operate solo. In 1984, the Pennekamp Coral Reef Institute (PCRI) was formed to support the park's mission.

On September 5, 1984, Budd wrote in his diary . . .

> At 7:30 pm met with my fellow directors of the Pennekamp Coral Reef Institute, and was promptly elected President and Chairman! It may turn out to be interesting . . . or else a real pain.

The Pennekamp Coral Reef Institute, Inc. was a private, non-profit organization, created in 1984. Its purpose was to "support the preservation and care of the Florida Keys Reef through assistance to the Marine Sanctuary and the John Pennekamp State Underwater Park. The Institute provides funding for mooring buoys, marine research, and education.

Furthermore, the Institute is composed of nine directors, who serve without compensation. As needs arise for action to fulfill the Institute purpose, the Board inaugurates fundraising, public awareness, and other support."

For almost 10 years, PCRI worked on a project close to Budd's heart—adapting the original living quarters and work areas at the Carysfort Reef Lighthouse to an offshore marine research facility . . .

Light meringue left behind as the Atlantic Ocean washed over the four-mile-long coral reef was evidence that *something* waited barely beneath the surface. Still, in 1770, corals snagged the hull of the British frigate, H.M.S. *Carrysford*. It could be the ship's name was bastardized. It could be it was roughly translated. No one told the story. We do know Carysfort Coral Reef is the namesake of the 28-gun, ill-fated British frigate.

Carysfort Coral Reef is one of the largest, most mature, coral reefs in Florida's almost 400-mile-long reef chain. Coral reefs create specialized habitats for Florida's unique plants and animals and lay the foundation for a dynamic ecosystem, with almost unsurpassed biodiversity. Reef maturation is slow. Some species grow only one-half inch per year.

In 1824, Congress allotted $20,000 to mark Carysfort Coral Reef with a lightship. The following year *Caesar* sailed from New York Harbor. Her oil lanterns were visible twelve miles out; her clanging bells echoed across rolling waves; her foghorn moaned—low . . . deep.

Caesar was bound for Carysfort Coral Reef, approximately six nautical miles off the coast of North Key Largo, on the southernmost tip of the Bermuda Triangle—an area of the North Atlantic Ocean where ships and aircraft reputedly disappear under *very* mysterious conditions.

Caesar's voyage didn't proceed exactly per plan—high winds and nasty seas drove her to shore near Key Biscayne, where her transport crew abandoned ship. Wreckers towed her to Key West, where she was salvaged, re-stocked, re-crewed, and re-positioned at Turtle Harbor—a safe anchorage near Carysfort Reef.

Six years into *Caesar's* service her captain, John Whalton, sailed her to Key West for inspection. It did not go well. The Collector of Customs reported that *Caesar's* timbers were "an entire mass of dry rot and fungus. I must say there was never a grosser imposition of a vessel succumbing to the environment. *Caesar* is doomed."

Congress allotted another $20,000 to build another lightship. Times had changed—*Florida* was constructed with rot-resistant live oak timber. Captain John Whalton resumed his post as commander. By then, Captain Whalton realized that he and his crew could not depend on supply ships for fresh fruits and vegetables. So, they planted a garden on North Key Largo.

On June 26, 1837, Captain Whalton and four crew members paddled ashore to tend their garden. They secured their dinghy. They unloaded their tools. But before they could even hoe the first weed, Seminole Indian warriors "harvested" their scalps. The attack marked the beginning of the Second Seminole War, and almost two hundred years later, the area near Mile Marker 106, on current day U.S.1/A1A is still known as *Garden Cove*.

So much for lightships. In 1848, Congress allocated funds for Carysfort Coral Reef's first permanent light. Carysfort

Reef Lighthouse is an iron pile structure, built with broad-bladed screws at the end of each foundation piling. It is the first of its kind in Florida.

In the early days, lighthouses didn't operate on their own. Men—*mortal* men—tended them. But, apparently, not solo. As the story goes, Carysfort Light's first ghost was a "great sinner" during his earthly life. Hoping to thwart off his devilish antics, lighthouse keepers slept with one eye (and their Bible) open.

Then, in 1927, Charles Bookfield, a Key Largo fisherman, spent a night at the Carysfort Light. Just after midnight, he was startled awake by a ghoulish shriek . . . once . . . twice. The third time, Charles grabbed his flashlight and bounded up the spiral staircase to the light room, where Keeper Jenks was working. "What in the world was that horrible noise?" he asked.

Jenks didn't even glance up from his logbook. "That's just old Captain Johnson. He died aboard the light and still comes around to keep me company."

In 1960, Carysfort Light was automated. Neither humans nor ghosts stuck around to maintain the beacon that, from 15 nautical miles out, warned mariners of Carysfort Reef's impending peril.

Bob Harris says . . .

Funny story about Carysfort Reef Lighthouse: PBS&J used the lighthouse as a survey point. Around late sixty-two or early sixty-three, we happened to be out there the same week they changed it over from one hundred thirty years of continuous manning to an automatic operation. In other words, they eliminated the lighthouse keeper.

Well, the lighthouse has a barrel, about a hundred and twenty feet across, at the bottom. We had to walk through that barrel to get up to the deck and set our survey points. And every single foot of that barrel was wallpapered with Playboy *centerfolds. I guess lighthouse keepers had to do SOMETHING to pass the time.*

Jimmy says . . .

Dad was president and then treasurer of the Pennekamp Coral Reef Institute. After Carysfort Reef Lighthouse was automated, the group was very interested in restoring its two-story living quarters and turning the lighthouse into a research station. It would have been the only permanent research station on a living coral reef in the world.

The institute members did everything imaginable to make it happen: they promoted it heavily; they made posters; they held big cocktail receptions as fundraisers. PBS&J even prepared detailed design plans.

But the Coast Guard refused to budge. The powers that be said, "NO! It's an operational lighthouse. It's ours. You can't have it!"

Budd wrote in his diary . . .

Another rainy, windy day—but getting better by late afternoon. Went to Cheeca Lodge for luncheon meeting/picture signing affair for PCRI. Dante Fascell, Tom Pennekamp, and Gary Burghoff ("Radar" of the M*A*S*H TV show) signed the 400 reproductions of Barry Barnetts' painting of the Carysfort Lighthouse. ("Radar" is now a permanent resident of Marathon—which is the basis for his selection. After lunch, and some general mingling (which gave me a chance to button-hole Dante about foreign affairs for about 10 minutes) and then a PCRI board meeting, which caught up the rest of the board about the grant application process ("slow") and our recent recon trip to the light. Also talked, later to Pete Perdue, who confirmed that things are in an uproar at OR with the new president and his hard nose policies about everything and everybody.

Talked this afternoon to Mike White, NOAA, and we agreed that the best way will be for NOAA grant for $200,000 for planning and design of the Carysfort Research Station should be channeled to the Pennekamp Coral Reef Institute for selection and contracting with the consultant. Hope PBSJ gets the job, but I pointed out to him the complications attending my presence on the

Board. His solution: just don't vote! The problem needs to be obviated long ahead of time.

Went to NOAA office and met with Tim Keeney and Jack Crowley of NOAA/Washington. Keeney (ex SEAL, etc.) is just under the NOAA director and is in charge of sanctuaries and is here partly in connection with the possible re-location of the submersible Aquarius from Puerto Rico to Pennekamp. Conversation with Crowley (who apparently is an engineer) indicates that it is not feasible to put a decompression chamber on the Carysfort Light lower deck. Weather, docking facilities make it undesirable—a waste of time and money to pursue. Instead, they are talking about a permanent reef research facility on shore with the Lighthouse facility simply a field station for observation/collection, possible with videotape observation.

We went to Fahrer's to pick up the finally arrived letter from NOAA proposing some kind of arrangement to begin to proceed to negotiate to commence to start some kind of action toward the development of the research facility on Carysfort Light.

Went to Alison Fahrer's house to meet with a NOAA representative for the DC office, to discuss, again, our application for the grant funds to do the engineering on the Carysfort project. She tells us, now, that it is too close to the end of the fiscal year (September 30) for any money to be spent this fiscal year. I pointed out that we were <u>begging</u> the local office for the application forms all Spring and that NOAA's delay has been the problem. It is my estimate that the plans will not be ready in time to take bids to get the work done next summer, during good weather. What a schedule!

Talked with Alison twice—told her that we are doomed to frustration on our lighthouse project unless we get the powers that be at the top of NOAA and the Coast Guard informed in detail as to what is being proposed (and what has been approved, implicitly by Congress as evidenced by the $200,000 grant in the 1991 budget) so that they in turn will tell all the ribbon clerks up and down the chain that the project must be permitted to proceed, subject to following the usual/normal rules of procedure.

Time passed. In 1993, the Coast Guard raised new obstacles. PCRI countered with a plea to Congress . . . "Break the impasse." No deal. Apparently, uncertain Federal support eliminated further major fundraising efforts.

As of 2014, the Carysfort Reef Lighthouse stands empty. A solitary, automated navigation beacon is its lonely legacy.

12.

Jack Reed

Ángel Castro y Argiz was a peasant, born in a small fieldstone house, typical of poor Galician peasants. In 1882, 17-year-old Ángel was recruited by the Spanish army and sent to Cuba to fight in its second War of Independence. The war ended. Time passed. Señor Argiz prospered. By the early 1920s, he owned a 23,000 acre sugar cane plantation—*Las Manacas*—in Birán, a village in the Holguín Province of Cuba.

Lina Ruz González was Señor Argiz's household servant. Frankly, his mistress. On August 13, 1926, the unmarried Señorita González gave birth to Señor Argiz's son. She named him Fidel Castro Ruz.

Fidel was not an easy child. When he was 6 years old, his mother sent him to Santiago de Cuba to live with his teacher and attend La Salle boarding school. Even nuns couldn't handle the boy. So, Fidel was sent away again. This time to Jesuit-run El Colegio de Belén in Havana, where he excelled in sports. Not academics.

In 1945, Fidel enrolled at the University of Havana to study law. Fidel's actual interest, though, was student activism and the violent *gangsterismo* culture within the university—a culture passionate about anti-imperialism—specifically, the United States' intervention in the Caribbean.

But anti-imperialism wasn't Fidel's only concern. In November 1946, he delivered a speech renouncing Cuban President Ramón Grau's government and Cuba's constitution. With that, 20-year-old Fidel Castro (now known simply as *Castro*) received heated public attention—attention that followed him the rest of his life.

During Castro's junior year at the university, he joined the Socialist Party of the Cuban people (*Partido Ortodoxo*). Violence erupted. Castro received death threats, demanding that he leave the university. He refused. Instead, he surrounded himself with armed friends, wielded a weapon, and continued to protest openly, via speeches delivered with a distinct leftist slant.

Influenced by Karl Marx, Friedrich Engels, and Vladimir Lenin, Castro believed Cuba's problems stemmed from bourgeoisie dictatorship, not corrupt politicians' shortcomings. Castro was convinced that meaningful political change would occur *only* through proletariat revolution.

Castro formed a group called *The Movement* and turned his beliefs into reality . . . In 1953, just hours before Castro and his brother, Raúl, led nearly two hundred rebels in a 6 a.m. attack on the Moncada Barracks (the first battle of the Cuban Revolution) Castro promised his followers,

> *"In a few hours you will be victorious or defeated, but regardless of the outcome—listen well, friends—this Movement will triumph. If we win tomorrow, the aspirations of Marti will be fulfilled sooner. If we fail, our action will nevertheless set an example for the Cuban people, and from the people, will arise fresh new men willing to die for Cuba."*

Following the attack, authorities rounded up the rebels. Some were tortured. Some were executed. Others, including self-proclaimed "revolutionary socialist" Fidel Castro, were transported to prison. During the 15 years Castro was imprisoned, he continued to read and strengthen his Marxist position. He continued to insist that he and his band of insurgents rose up against Cuban dictator Fulgencio Batista y Zaldívar because he had "seized power in an unconstitutional manner."

In 1954, Castro wrote, *"I would honestly love to revolutionize this country from one end to the other! I am sure this would bring happiness to the Cuban people. I would not be stopped by the hatred and ill will of a few thousand people."*

After Castro was released from prison, he strengthened his relationship with The Movement (now called *MR-26-7*). Some already labeled him a *caudillo* (dictator). Castro, himself, argued that a successful revolution could not be run by a committee. It required a strong leader.

In early 1955, Castro befriended a Marxist-Leninist named Ernesto "Che" Guevara and Che's associate, Alberto Bayo. The two, who were revolutionaries in their own right, taught Castro and his revolutionaries guerrilla warfare tactics. Castro set up camp in the thickly forested Sierra Maestra mountain range. His troops launched raids. Batista and his army countered with torture and extrajudicial executions.

Cuba's neighbor, 90 miles north, was appalled and, frankly, embarrassed. U.S. Senator John F. Kennedy said,

> *"Fulgencio Batista murdered twenty thousand Cubans in seven years ... and he turned Democratic Cuba into a complete police state—destroying every individual liberty. Yet our aid to his regime, and the ineptness of our policies, enabled Batista to invoke the name of the United States in support of his reign of terror.*
>
> *Administration spokesmen publicly praised Batista— hailed him as a staunch ally and a good friend— at a time when Batista was murdering thousands, destroying the last vestiges of freedom, and stealing hundreds of millions of dollars from the Cuban people, and we failed to press for free elections. I believe there is no country in the world including any and all the countries under colonial domination, where economic colonization, humiliation, were worse than in Cuba, in part owing to my country's policies during the Batista regime."*

With that, the United States imposed an arms embargo on Batista's government. And Cuban dictator, Fulgencio Batista (along with 300 million U.S. dollars), fled into exile.

Castro ordered the MR-26-7 to halt looting and vandalism. Then, accompanied by cheering crowds, he marched into Havana, where he proclaimed that Manuel Urrutia Lleó was Cuba's Provisional President and Fidel Castro was its Representative of the Rebel Armed Forces of the Presidency.

As Urrutia's right-hand man, Castro insisted on implementing policies that cut corruption and fought illiteracy. He repeatedly (but falsely) claimed the Urrutia regime would hold multiparty elections. Although Castro assured the press that he was not a communist, he attended clandestine meetings with the Popular Socialist Party. *Surely*, Cubans would prosper as citizens of a socialist country.

Time passed. Castro was sworn in as Prime Minister of Cuba and appointed Marxists to senior government and military positions. His radio and television "dialogue with the people" appearances promised Cubans that their standard of living would improve. Castro's ideology was popular with workers, peasants, and students. The middle class, though, flocked to Florida. Brain drain was rampant. Financial reserves disappeared. The conservative press was hostile. People worldwide wanted answers—now.

In "explanation," Castro's forces arrested hundreds of counter-revolutionaries and subjected them to solitary confinement and harsh—inhumane—treatment. Militant anti-Castro groups (many funded by the United States' Central Intelligence Agency—the CIA) set up guerrilla bases in Cuban's mountains. The six-year War Against the Bandits raged. The Cold War between the world's two superpowers—the United States of America (a capitalist country, founded on Democracy) and the Soviet Union (a socialist state, ruled by the Communist Party)—intensified.

And Castro? Well, Castro agreed to supply the Soviet Union with sugar, fiber, and hides in return for crude oil, fertilizers, industrial goods, and a $100 million loan. He then ordered Cuba's refineries—refineries that were controlled by U.S. corporations—to process Soviet oil. They refused. No problem. Castro seized the operations and declared them, "state-owned."

Once again, Cuba's neighbor, 90 miles north, was appalled, but this time NOT embarrassed. In retaliation, the United States refused to import Cuban sugar. So, Castro nationalized sugar mills and announced that Cuba had officially adopted the Soviet's model of rule. With that, Cuba became a single-party state; the government controlled trade unions; civil liberties vanished; freedom of speech disappeared. "Up north" the anti-Castro movement strengthened.

Time passed. During the latter months of 1960, a young senator from Massachusetts was briefed on a top-secret CIA plan, developed by Dwight D. Eisenhower's administration. After all, on January 20, 1961, John F. Kennedy—JFK— would be inaugurated as the 35th president of the United States of America. He needed to know.

JFK learned that the CIA's plan included training Cuban exiles to storm their homeland via the Bay of Pigs and anticipated that the Cuban people and certain elements of the Cuban military would support the invasion. The plan's ultimate goal was to overthrow Castro and establish a non-communist government, friendly to the United States. José Miró Cardona (a former leader of the Cuban Revolutionary Council) was already poised to take over as Cuba's provisional president.

Regardless of high-level intelligence efforts to keep the plan covert, the press leaked suspicions. Still, the by-now President Kennedy authorized it to proceed, provided he could disguise U.S. support. After all, the remote, swampy Bay of Pigs itself was part of the deception. Further, two surprise strikes against Cuban air bases, followed by a fourteen-hundred-man invasion force, disembarking under the cover of darkness, followed by a smaller secret force, creating confusion on the opposite coast was failsafe. Wasn't it?

Well, as the saying goes, *the best-laid plans* . . .

The first mishap occurred April 15, 1961, when eight obsolete, World War II, B-26 bombers headed toward Cuban airfields. They missed most targets. Castro's air force remained intact. United States' involvement was exposed. President Kennedy cancelled the second air strike.

On April 17, the U.S. Cuban-exile invasion force, known as *Brigade 2506,* landed on beaches along the Bay of Pigs. Cuban planes shelled the invaders, destroyed half their air support, and sank two escort ships. The ground force was hampered by bad weather, soggy equipment, and insufficient ammunition.

Over the next 24 hours, as the Cuban air force controlled the skies, Castro ordered over 20,000 homeland troops to advance toward the beach. President Kennedy hung on by authorizing six unmarked fighter planes to defend America's waning position. They arrived one hour too late. Cubans shot them down.

Many were killed. Some escaped to the sea. Over 1,200 surrendered. United States dignitaries attempted to negotiate a release-deal. Nothing. Finally, United States Attorney General Robert F. Kennedy stepped in, and Castro exchanged American prisoners for $53 million worth of baby food and medicine.

And on October 19, 1986—25 years after he was captured— Ramon Conte Hernández, Brigade 2506's last prisoner, stepped off a plane onto home soil.

Flashbulbs popped. Reporters shoved microphones in his face. Mr. Hernández faced the whirring TV cameras. He smiled. He said, "My ideas have not changed. It is difficult to retire from the struggle for freedom—the struggle against communism."

Flashback to 1962. JFK's troubles were not over . . .

In May 1962, the Soviet Union's Premier Nikita Khrushchev offered to position Soviet nuclear missiles in Cuba. *Surely*, nuclear weapons would protect the island from future invasions. By late summer, Castro and Khrushchev reached a secret agreement. Missile site construction proceeded silently, yet swiftly.

Well, not all secrets are *secrets*. JFK's newly created Defense Intelligence Agency was suspicious. So, on October 14, 1962, a United States Air Force U-2 scanned suspected areas and shot photographs of medium- and intermediate-range nuclear missiles.

Early morning October 15, President Kennedy organized ExComm (his twelve most trusted advisors) to discuss the situation, turned crisis. The men debated for seven days. On October 22, the news went public, and Kennedy announced his decision to impose a naval "quarantine" (actually, a military blockade) around Cuba. Risky, in itself.

Even more risky, Kennedy asserted that any nuclear missile launched from Cuba would be interpreted as a direct attack on the United States. He, then, demanded that the Soviets dismantle and remove their offensive weapons—immediately.

Khrushchev responded with a letter stating, "Navigation in international waters and airspace constituted an act of aggression propelling humankind into the abyss of a nuclear-missile world war."

Top-secret negotiations between the two world leaders flew back and forth across continents, over and under ideologies, in and around world destruction.

In the meantime, Soviet ships attempted to run the blockade. United States Navy ships were ordered to fire warning shots. Then, open fire. On October 27, a United States U-2 was shot down by a Soviet missile crew. *Was this really the end of the world?* Kennedy and Khrushchev continued deliberating.

On October 28, President Kennedy and United Nations Secretary General U Thant reached an agreement with Premier Khrushchev . . . The Soviet Union agreed to dismantle their weapons in Cuba and return them to the Soviet Union; the United States agreed to state formally that it would never invade Cuba.

It was close . . . very close . . . too close. But when all was said and done, nuclear war was averted. The world breathed a sigh of relief.

Still, could American's *really* trust Fidel Castro? Was the anti-Castro movement *really* over? In 1964, Floridians in 40 counties were queried by the *Miami Herald, St. Petersburg Times, Florida Times-Union,* and *Lake Wales Highlander*: "What, if anything, do you think the United States should do about Cuba and Fidel Castro?"

Miami Herald reporter, Don Bohning, of the Latin American staff, summarized: "Floridians are fed up with Cuba under Fidel Castro, but few are ready to risk an all-out U.S. invasion of the island as a solution."

Then, there was Budd Post, secretly known as "Jack Reed."

Jack Read, a.k.a. "Budd Post"

Budd recorded his involvement in the anti-Castro movement in his diary . . .

Sunday, February 2, 1964

> Jimmy's birthday is tomorrow so we had a little party today. I cooked hot dogs in the backyard for him and 5 friends—then took them downtown where I picked up and delivered to Rogelio [member of the Cuban Revolutionary Assembly] two combat boot samples.

In explanation: Rogelio Cisneros was the Chief in Exile of the Revolutionary Junta—JURE. Manuel Ray founded JURE. Both were involved with secret, guerrilla military action against Fidel Castro.

Budd continued writing in his diary . . .

Sunday, May 3, 1964

> Spent almost all day, till 3:00, paying bills balancing checking account, etc. Then picked up Jaime and we went to the meeting of the Junta Directorate, which has been in progress for two days. We attended as invited guests, and I consider it to be somewhat of an honor. All 7 of the Directors in exile were present and we met in the Wesley Foundation Building at the University of Miami arranged thru the good offices of Rev. Rivas, Methodist Preacher & Junta director!
>
> The principal discussion concerned my idea previously presented by Jaime & Rogelio to organize Americans to support JURE. The consensus seemed to favor the idea, so we shall wait and see. . . . This is the last time Manuel Ray will be in the States; he will be in Cuba before May 20 1964 and Gomez, a labor leader, will go with him. And now to push the explosives course!

No surprise, Budd's explosives' course (three sessions to be exact) was precise. Detailed. Written out word for word in English *and* Spanish . . .

Good Evening. My name is "Jill," and I will be your instructor for a three-hour course in rudimentary demolitions. The purpose of this course is to teach you the very minimum skills that you must have in order to safely and successfully detonate a simple explosive charge using non-electric means.

You have been given an outline of this course of instruction along with demolition cards, and these demolition cards contain in a condensed form a great deal of information and knowledge about military explosives and demolitions, and before this course is over, we hope that you will understand most of the information on these cards.

Our first class will be devoted to a general consideration of explosives, what they are, how you use them, how they are manufactured, how you should handle them, how you should store them, the safety precautions, what it takes to detonate them, etc. The second hour will be devoted to a practical application of what you have learned, and we expect that each of you will detonate one small practice charge so that you will know how it really feels. The third hour will be devoted to ways and means in which you might be able to employ explosives and then the last thing will be an examination to see whether or not you have successfully mastered the information that we will present to you.

Let us begin . . .

Budd continued writing in his diary . . .

Tuesday, May 5, 1964

> Picked up 8 pair of cap crimping pliers today . . . everything seems to be moving in the right direction. After supper completed exam for Field Fortifications sub-course.

May 19, 1964

> After lunch in Lauderdale went to see Rogelio. He unloaded a real surprise. Wants me to arrange the boat to carry Ray to a rendezvous at Orange Cay Thursday! I'm in high gear now! Saw Dick Mooney and Giff Bunnell and they are working on it—in strict secrecy and only fragmentary information, of course.

May 20, 1964

Didn't go to the office today; instead, spent all morning making frantic telephone calls trying to line up a suitable boat. Finally went to Bertram's about 1:30 and chartered a 25 ft. twin 110 mer-cruiser Bertram. Went to office at 3:00 and met with Goldberg & Weiss of Pix shoes—looks like they are ready to go ahead.

Met Rogelio and Rudy at office at 1900 and discussed the project—as of now. I am to go tomorrow from Bertram's to Venetian Isle Motel in my chartered 25 footer. Allen Gray is coming down to crew for me (and captain really!) tomorrow afternoon. The Cuban captain will come aboard and familiarize himself. Then Friday AM we will take off to rendezvous at Orange Kay, from whence Ray will make the dash.

Venetian Motel - May 64

Revolutionary's transport

In May 1964, Manuel Ray and Rogelio Cisneros wrote a letter to the Cuban Revolutionary Assembly . . .

Cuban Revolutionary Assembly

P.O BOX 35-158

Miami, Florida

1878 W Flagler

Miami 35, Florida

May 1964

Proclamation of May 20th

From the Cuban Revolutionary Assembly (JURE) to the People of Cuba:

A new war of independence has commenced in Cuban soil. After less than five years from what was the dawn of national hope, the communist usurpation, insulated into power by treason, has violated all rights, submerged the people into misery, destroyed the wealth of the country, implanted totalitarian terror, and has placed in foreign hands the destiny of the nation.

The tragic deeds of the communist tyrant will now come to an end. The people's victory does not come in the form of spectacular invasions nor with anti-patriotic alliances. It moves forward with the progressive mobilization of the people by way of an insurrectional movement: The Cuban Revolutionary Assembly (JURE), created to organize and develop the resistance and to conduct the nation towards the democratic forces of the triumph of liberation.

This is a new war that we have not provoked. The only responsible parties of this war are those who betrayed the revolutionary ideals that had inspired the Cuban people in their heroic struggle against the Batista dictatorship. It is a war against the Soviet empire and its people's bondage. It is a war against hunger, against misery, against terror. It is a war for freedom, for justice, for reason. We are not moved by resentment, hate or revenge. On the contrary, we assert love and understanding, solidarity and greatness. We would not be worthy of our glorious ancestors if the ambition of power, or the desire to overcome assumed or real grievances would be what has moved us to summon the people to armed force.

This war must be waged by all Cubans of morals, regardless of the position they occupy or the uniform they wear. The deceived military man, the betrayed soldier, the state employee, all have the duty to respond to the call of the homeland, joining the fight against the communist usurpation. Our rifles are not pointed against them, but to those who by betraying the Cuban people as a whole, have betrayed them as well.

We do not wage this war either to re-establish privileges or social injustices. This war is waged to destroy oppressive communism and to create a prosperous democratic society, that distributes wealth and not misery, where the empire of the law and equality of opportunity for all may enjoy its maximum expression. If we cannot build this society with a profound democratic content in which political, social and economic order prevail, there will always be a sector of the population that will rise against it or that will live resentfully in such society.

We believe in the fundamental equality of all human beings. We are disgusted by racial discrimination, and we fight for eliminating the social inequalities that this has created.

This is a struggle of the Cubans in defense of its more vital and legitimate interests. This is the struggle of the peasants, to obtain their own land. It is the struggle of the workers for the freedom to defend their participation in national production. It is the struggle of the farmers, entrepreneurs and industrialists to shake off the chains that impede them from offering their contribution to the economy of the nation. It is the struggle of students and professionals for freedom of culture. It is the struggle of women for the integrity of their home, divided by hate and subjected to hunger. It is the struggle of all men to profess their religion, and to profess their political rights that have been taken from them. It is the struggle of all Cubans for a life free of fear and misery.

We were, we are, and we will continue to be revolutionaries. Revolution is reconstruction, not the trampling of rights, nor the distribution of hunger. Revolution is justice, not the teasing of human dignity, nor unpunished murder. Because of the betrayal of the revolution we summon the people to this new war of independence. This is what thousands of fallen martyrs deserve, who have fallen in the strife of the last twelve years, who have been represented in the sublime and selfless figure of the immortal Frank Pais. Cuba cannot allow that the historic sacrifice of so many martyrs be in vain. To their blood shed we must add the blood shed which must be necessary to redeem them.

To our rebel military brothers of the clandestine fight, that risked their lives with us, suffered with us and conquered the triumph with us, over the criminal usurpation of March 10th, to them, our old peers that today disappointedly contemplate the betrayal, we say to them time has come to take up the arms again against tyranny.

Worker unions of Latin America have given us their moral and material support. Organizations of professors and university students have been founded in the hemisphere to defend the true Cuban Revolution. We have on our side the opinion of the democratic America, which feel as if it were their own, the physical and moral damages imposed on our people by the communist tyranny, with the same solidarity with which we reject the tyrannies that are still plaguing other parts of the continent.

A feat of glorious dimensions is in front of the Cuban people: that of destroying the myth of their inability of liberating itself which was imposed by the communist tyrant in order to attain perpetual power. The Cuban people are not less powerful today than they were when they shook off the colonial chains and cast off the power of the two satraps which preceded the communist tyrant. Our heroic tradition must be fulfilled relentlessly, by historical mandate and because bayonets are insufficient to maintain those who display lies as the basis of power, the hypocrisy as a government system, and terror as revolutionary work.

We want a homeland in which true friendship, family love and mutual trust will be re-born, the mutilated values of the communist usurpation. A homeland which will march as indicated by Marti and Bolivar, next to its American brothers.

We declare solemnly that once the communist tyranny has fallen, we shall abolish the death sentence. With a triumphant democratic revolution, brutality and the firing squad wall shall be abolished.

Cuba shall be free.

FOR A CUBAN CUBA,
By the Directive of JURE:

Manuel Ray

Rogelio Cisneros

Budd continued writing in his diary . . .

Thursday, May 21, 1964

> Allen arrived at 0800—on schedule. Completed charter formalities and left Bertram's at 0915. Reached Venetian Isles Motel at 1100—no sweat. Took cab to Bertram's to pick up car; then home for lunch, then back to boat to await word. Rudy came by about 3:30 and said plans were changed—nothing for me until 1500 tomorrow. Allen and I took boat out to try her out—good show—except port lower unit is overheating.

Saturday, May 23, 1964

Spent morning in office—mostly completing exam for "Nuclear Weapons Employment." Am glad to have that over with. Went to Venetian Isles Motel at noon and Rogelio arrived about 1300 with Rudy—operations called off for bad weather and other difficulties.

Sunday, May 24, 1964

Rudy called at 1600 and arrived at 1630. We made a quick run out to the sea to familiarize him with the boat; he will be running it if needed this coming week. Talked to Rogelio at 1900 at his house, and then Rudy took me home. I know for sure:

1. Manuel Ray has to get into Cuba soon
2. The Junta is buying and equipping a 31' Bertram which will be held in my name— for my use—and their use on special occasions.

Wednesday, May 27, 1964

Don't remember the details during the day, but met Rogelio & Rudy at the office at 1900. Was surprised when they told me that Manuel was in room 109 at the Venetian Isle Motel. I took him some supper and talked to him for about an hour—he was surprise to see me because I am apparently the only American in the operation. He was in good spirits, calm, relaxed, and was going to read the Engineering News Record I left with him when I departed about 2230. Sure hope he makes it.

Thursday, May 28, 1964

Manuel left the Venetian Isle Motel this morning at 0900. If all goes will he will land in Cuba tonight.

Friday, May 29, 1964

Went to Bertram's at 0900 and found that Rudy had returned the chartered Bertram 25—damaged somewhat. I told them it was all done without my knowledge and I'll have to submit a couple of statements for the insurance company. Met Rogelio at the office at noon and he said that no news was good news—so far the boat carrying Manuel is expected back about 1800 today.

Arrived home about 1600 and had urgent call to see Rogelio. The operation was hung up. The boat reached an isolated key 60 miles from Cuba and 78 miles from Tavernier. Gas consumption was excessive and speed to slow so Manuel and 5 others were left on the key and the boat came back to Tavernier. The trouble was that the boat was vastly overloaded. I'm to try to locate a bigger boat with more power, but the holiday, etc. will make it difficult.

Saturday, May 30, 1964

Worked around the house doing minor chores all day, with time out to try to locate a suitable boat to get Manuel into Cuba. As expected everything is closed. Manuel, the girl (Rogelio's ward), the Life photographer, and the two men who are to guide the party once they get ashore are stranded still on the deserted key where they were Thursday.

Sunday, May 31, 1964

Home all day except for early church. Heard nothing from Rogelio, so I think they are making the move today. Hit a couple of buckets of balls at Miami Lakes with Jeanne & Jimmy about 5:00. Finished another sub-course, by exam only, tonite.

Wednesday, June 3, 1964

Headed for GRC meeting about 1430 and stopped at Rogelio's for an urgent message—a British destroyer picked up Manuel and party. I had to leave to go to the GRC meeting and while there had to stand up and point the finger at the highway engineering branch and say private enterprise can do it cheaper. After supper met Rogelio at the office and after much talk, long distance telephone calls, etc. I am to go to Nassau in the morning to try to help Manuel et. al.

Thursday, June 4, 1964

Caught the 0830 PAA jet, carrying $1,000 in twenty dollar bills. Took a room ($209) at the Carlton House and then joined the photographer and newsmen out in front of the police station.

The police kept everyone back. Manuel tried to hide, and the hearing started on the upstairs room in Ranfierly. About 5 minutes later the CBS man came running out—and although he wouldn't say, I am sure he was running to flash the identification of Manuel.

The hearing started about 1030 and by noon they were back in the central police station. I finally got in to see him as "Jack Reed with Andrew St. George's money from Travellers Express." and after milling around, Manuel and I stepped out the back door, thru an alley, into the Carlton House. I spent some time trying to locate a boat to carry the party to Miami—but no soap. Finally left and caught Bahama Airways 1700 flight to Miami.

Watched Jimmy graduate from kindergarten at the church, and then met with Rogelio for almost 3 hours; he is assembling the directorate to decide what to do next.

Sunday, June 14, 1964

Early church and then a short meeting with Rogelio at 10:00. Nothing special for me to do at present. Next effort to get Manuel into Cuba will not be from US.

Tuesday, June 16, 1964

Met with Rogelio today and he wants me to go to Jamaica to check out a potential site for launching Manuel . . . "Blue Hole." Will go Friday.

Friday, June 19, 1964

Left on PAA jet at 0800 for Kingston, Jamaica via Montego Bay. Then rented a car (Anglia) for the 75 mile drive to the vicinity of Port Antonio on the north coast (via road A-4). Found "Blue Lagoon" which is name of bar-restaurant that Robin Moore has built on his property at Blue Hole. He wasn't available at the moment, so went on in to Port Antonio and registered at the Bonnie View Hotel, on top of the hills overlooking the harbor. Met Moore about 5:00 and identified myself and we started talking. He has many assets for JURE, but he has weaknesses too. Had dinner with him and his fiancée, Margo Palmer and her mother Rita in the cottage overlooking Blue Hole, where they are staying as his house guests. Then back to the Bonnie View for a nite cap, which nobody needed and I didn't want.

Saturday, June 20, 1964

Checked out and met Moore again at 1130 and talked some more, looked at potential housing for people, and then departed for Kingston at 1:30; plane left at 1800, and home about 2500.

Sunday, June 28, 1964

Jamie called to tell me that the FBI had come to the Keys house and told Mateo to move the radio equipment immediately—no questions asked.

Monday, June, 29, 1964

> Routine day at the office, except a call from Al
> Burt of the Herald asking about my Nassau trip
> for JURE and indicating, by his conversation, that
> people have been talking. I didn't deny the story
> about being in Nassau, but I didn't tell him much
> else—but I'll guarantee it will be all screwed up
> if ever printed.

Robin Moore's Jamaican estate

Friday, July 10, 1964

> Rogelio and Ray came to the office this morning
> at 0730—R is just back from Dominican Republic.
> Said he was leaving today for another attempt to
> reach Cuba.

Sunday, August 2, 1964

> Early church, Sunday School and fried chicken
> for lunch. Jimmy went over to Mom's about 3:00

to spend the night. Met with Allen Gray, Manuel Ray, and Bebo Acosta and Manuel Varila in office at 2:00 and discussed boat (Bertram) until 2300. Guess it will get underway now.

That's it. Not one more word from Budd Post, a.k.a. "Jack Reed." We're left hanging. What happened?

When Budd was alive, he didn't talk about "Jack Reed's" activities, even to his family. Jeanne says that a reporter once called Budd a "steely-eyed CIA agent." But that's all she knows.

We can't ask Manuel Ray—he died November 12, 2014.

To find out what happened we turn to the Internet. Wikipedia to be exact . . .

In 1963-65, the JURE organized several actions against the Castro government. In the last of these actions, Ray along with several members of the JURE, was arrested at Anguila Cay in the Cay Sal Bank by the Bahamian Coast Guard. The group was using the small deserted island as a staging area for attacks against Cuba. The Bahamian government confiscated all weapons and supplies and briefly jailed the group, who eventually was deported back to the U.S.

After the arrest, Ray returned to Puerto Rico and to his professional career as an engineer. He ceased his involvement in armed actions against the Castro government, but continued political activities against the Castro regime. However, Mr. Ray became increasingly involved in Puerto Rican civic and political activities, serving as ad-honorem advisor to Governors Rafael Hernández Colón and Aníbal Acevedo Vilá, Mayor Héctor Luis Acevedo and gubernatorial candidate Victoria Muñoz Mendoza.

In 1967, along with Juan L. Melendez, former head of the Cuban water and sewer agency, he founded an engineering firm in San Juan, Puerto Rico. The firm, Ray Architects and Engineers, has been involved in multiple projects in Puerto Rico and the Caribbean. After retirement following a stroke in 1999, Ray served as the company's chairman emeritus.

Due to his contributions to Puerto Rican society, Ray was awarded the Luis Muñoz Marín medal by the government of Puerto Rico in the early 2000s.

So, as Paul Harvey once said, "Now you know the rest of the story . . . Good Day."

13.

'Til the Very End

Every disease has a history. Sometimes, when you least expect it, life smacks you, and you find yourself drawn to its discovery . . .

As far back as the ninth century, BCE, the Maxims of the Ptah Holy in Egypt identified a form of "unusual, forgetful behavior." Then, around 70, CE, Claudius Galen, a Roman physician, described symptoms of age-related forgetfulness in his diary. By the 1300s, the English had developed a verbal test to check for forgetfulness. But it wasn't until the early 1900s that the disease had a name.

In 1901, 51-year-old "Auguste D." was admitted to the state asylum in Frankfort, Germany. Among other maladies, she suffered from an unusual form of amnesia—frankly, "strange behavior." After Aguuste D. died in 1906, physician, Alois Alzheimer and psychiatrist, Emil Kraepelin studied her brain and discovered atrophied gray matter alongside unfamiliar bundles of neurofibers and plaques.

Dr. Alzheimer presented their scientific findings to a conference of psychiatrists and subsequently published a paper. In 1910, Dr. Kraepelin coined the term "Alzheimer's disease." In 1977, neurologist, Dr. Robert Katzman, declared Alzheimer's disease to be "the most common form of dementia and a substantial public health problem."

The Alzheimer's Foundation defines the disease as "a progressive, degenerative disorder that attacks the brain's nerve cells, resulting in loss of memory, thinking and language skills, and behavioral changes." Symptoms include the four As of Alzheimer's: Amnesia (memory loss); Aphasia (inability to communicate effectively); Apraxia (inability to perform normal activities of daily living); Agnosia (inability to interpret sensory signals).

Alzheimer's is one of the most researched diseases in the world. The Alzheimer's Association, alone, has awarded over $100 million in grants. Still, in 2014, even though this sinister disease is rapidly approaching epidemic proportions, there is no cure.

Intellectual, maybe.

Interesting, probably.

Important, definitely.

But what does it *mean* to Budd Post, his family, and his friends?

Budd's paradise and his best friend

Jeanne says . . .

> *I can't say for certain, but I think Budd inherited Alzheimer's from his mother—that's possible, you know. Jean had dementia real bad, so she ended up in the Miami Springs Villa and seemed happy enough there. It was within walking distance of our home, so we went to see her almost every day. And let me tell you, she gave those nurses hell.*

Budd wrote in his diary . . .

> Mom's birthday today—79! She got flowers from El and cards & candy from us—she is in good fireball spirits, but her memory is bad and her ability to walk gradually deteriorating.

Jeanne continues . . .

Alzheimer's is impossible to understand. Budd was the smartest guy I ever knew, but he ended up with Alzheimer's. Why? I can't begin to say. When we first noticed it, he started forgetting things—no big deal, everybody does that. Then it got worse and worse.

The really strange thing about Budd's Alzheimer's is he knew he had it (most people don't). And that's the one and only time in his entire life that he was scared—real scared. We tried to get treatment, but even a specialist couldn't do anything for him. At first, he lived at home, and I took care of him. Eventually, we moved to Tampa, and that's when I put Budd in a facility because, by then, he took off on his own real regular, and I was afraid he might get up in the middle of the night, wander off, and get hit by a car.

Budd was never fat and wasn't particularly interested in food. But right 'til the end, he loved his ice cream. Every night he sat in his chair and ate butterscotch ice cream and drank coffee. And no one DARED interrupt him.

In 1998, Budd was long retired from PBS&J. For whatever reason, he didn't keep in touch with anyone—even those who had been close to him when they worked together. Still, he wanted to go to the annual stockholders meeting, so Jimmy and I took him. People were shocked. They could hardly believe a man who had always been so smart and charismatic—a man who had always been so alert and such a great leader—a man who had always been such a generous mentor—couldn't even remember their names. Seeing Budd like that was tough on everyone. Basically, devastating.

The end of 68 years in the same house. Off to Tampa.

It wasn't that difficult to take care of Budd. I accepted it as a part of life. Of course, I was sorry to see him decline—he got worse and worse as weeks passed. One day, he was in a golf tournament and lined up like he was playing croquet. That's when I knew he had it real bad.

Budd had always been a great reader. He read hundreds of books—books of all types. He even kept notes on his books. I think some of his notes said more about him than he ever shared—with anyone. Even when Budd's Alzheimer's was real bad, he read every day.

Budd wrote in his diary . . .

The Lion of Wall Street—Jack Dreyfus

The author is the Wall Street Dreyfus, and his autobiography is interesting—because of his golf anecdotes. He is an excellent player—beat Sam Byrd in a tournament in Montgomery, Ala., was NY state amateur champ . . . but his book is a propaganda handout for the magical medical properties of Dilantin—He also mentions Dick Chapman—who beat him in a club tournament. He also mentions Alf Robertson. I met and played a couple times with Dick Chapman (when he was U.S. amateur champ in 1941 (?) at the Biltmore—his personal pro was Leo Walper who dad knew. Walper told me that Dad was supposed to meet him in Atlanta to play golf on his way back from Raleigh—but Dads northbound flight ended up in the Everglades crash!

Good Evening Everybody . . . and so long until tomorrow!—Lowell Thomas

A fascinating, nostalgic book for me because I can remember listening to him as a little kid (in New Jersey!) and how the grown-ups laughed when I called him "Local" Thomas! The book is a fascinating history of events that I heard about life—and now read about! World War I and Lawrence of Arabia—and the gold rush in California and Alaska—early airplane flights—will urge Jim to read it.

Contesting Castro—Thomas G. Paterson

A detailed description of the Castro revolution from the viewpoint of an American academic who clearly identifies with Castro and against Batista—and who didn't change his opinion about Castro in spite of what happened! He names several Cubans whom I met or know of through Rogelio and Ray. Based on my experiences and readings most all of the Cubans were anti-Batista (and thus, pro-Castro) until Castro revealed his true colors—and then they turned against him—but with the great majority (numerically) really unable to do much about it. An important addition to my library.

Only Yesterday—Frederick Lewis Allen

The book describes the decade of the 20s—and I have childhood memories of our house from the time I was about 5 years old. The stock market crash was the climax—and the numbers were staggering! His comments on the changes in sexual mores and attitudes and the violence of the Prohibition gangsters has a remarkable resemblance to the current changes in sex/violence attitudes—but we seem to have reached even greater peaks/lows today; there are two fundamental changes: 1. The explosion in communications and 2. The ever-increasing multiplication of the population. It bodes evil for the future!

Cool Hand Luke—Donn Pearce

A small novel about life on a Fla. chain gang along about the 50's—at which time I was working for the SRD, and had one encounter with the system when one of the chain gangs delivered the portable field "office" to our regular field office on NW 153rd St. We were renting a store front adjacent to Joe Brach's Machine Shop, and needed the shed for storage of supplies—such as stakes, tripods, boots, junk . . . The chain gang loaded and unloaded the building (12X16) from the flatbed trailer onto the "foundation" by hand, coordinated by the head colored guy shouting "Mule Train!" as he snatched his cap off and on when spoken to.

A Time of Change—Harrison Salisbury

An ego-trip autobiography covering Salisbury's travels, scoops, coups, meetings with the greats and lamentations over the failure with the greats to see the truth = take his advice. I used to think he was very good—an acute observer—such as "The 900 Days—The Siege of Leningrad" but in this book he discloses all the liberal traits that have always turned me against the NY Times and convinces me that my misgivings about the Times were well-founded. Classic example: "I revere (!) men like Seymour Hersh who reported the reality of Viet Nam."

<u>The Last Lion—Winston Spencer Churchill</u>—Wm. Manchester

It was absolutely fascinating! and a tremendous history lesson. Manchester's style of writing is absorbing, although the "personalization" and apparent "quotations" as if he were there are a little suspect, it makes it eminently readable. The view of World War I was most educational, as a result I read "First Day on the Somme" by Martin Middlebrook—1971 and am finally beginning to understand WWI a little better— especially the unique state of mind that must have gripped those fighting "the war to end all wars"—including my parents!

<u>Fall From Grace</u>—Fenton Bailey

A newspaper writer's rather extensive investigation of the whole affair—and the conclusion that I draw is that this was an unique event, the legal resolution of which was not fair to Milken, but which was so confusing and tangled and filled with so many lies and conflicting stories, that there could have been no "solution." Milken appears to be a mathematical genius—but the concept of leveraged buy-outs and junk bonds seems to me to be too sophisticated and hypothetical as to be unsuited for the general market-place. Honesty and hard work is still the usual way to succeed! People who make millions on a single transaction—and who deal in billions—are not of this world.

Jeanne continues . . .

Until the very end, Budd did his best to keep up his diary.

During 1998, Budd wrote in his diary . . .

I wish I could develop a feel for writing a diary that would be of interest to Jim and his family and Jeanne in years to come. But the way it appears to go is a simple bean-counter's approach to record trivia. But I do remember I love my house.

Watched the Rose Bowl football on TV (and now can't remember who won—Southern Cal or—"the opponent"—which is a significant sign/ symptom of my Alzheimer's I'm afraid. What a sorry way to start the New Year!!!

Brought back to M.S. the rifle and shotgun that I have kept in WS elevator shaft for the last several years without ever taking them out. I may as well give them to Jim because when I sighted thru the rifle sights my eye told me instantly that I had a problem! My eyes have changed considerable since the last time I sighted a weapon.

Golf at Riviera—had 83 and can't remember the names of the two guys I played with! (Never met/ saw them before, but still!!!) We son $45 apiece for low net. I do remember that.

Went to Riviera and putted and hit sand shots for an hour or so. Can't hit full shot because I have now developed a painful crick in the lower back (right side). Called golf course this morning and told them I was not going to play in the Senior's Tournament. I forfeited several hundred dollars in entry fees and travel expenses, but I just don't want to face 3 days of golf with total strangers when I'm in this condition. No confidence—it's just gone.

Memory gradually getting worse—Example: names escape me. Example: have difficulty remembering how long ago certain things happened—such as how many years we have been members of Rivera? I have "known" people at Riviera for a long time and still can't remember names. Example: How many years since I retired from PBSJ?

Finished reading <u>Citizen's Soldiers</u> by Stephen Ambrose, and it is **<u>excellent</u>**, in my biased views. It describes WWII thru the eye of a young soldier who was jerked out of Army Specialized Training Program, which includes me, Warren Schelling, Jim Scott, PV and numerous other friends. I sure remember those days.

Jim just called—no spectacular news or anything, but it is nice to be able to talk to him and I'm glad he called.

I still watch the news—all the news media are currently focused on Pres. Clinton's adventures with Monica Lewinski—for my part, I think he is a real shit, who will do whatever he wants to do and will say anything he thinks will help him— whether it is true or not. He is an excellent speaker, smart, etc., but utterly without scruples—and his wife is brilliant, and just as unscrupulous!!!

Jeanne & I took off for a little shopping today. Jeanne laid into me today over my forgetfulness about where we were going—and I'm afraid it will only get worse—don't have a contingency plan for when the fateful day arrives when I won't be able to drive alone for fear of getting "lost" or something similar. SWELL.

Tonite I showed Jeanne six half pair of socks and complained that Teresa must have lost the other six halves. (Not the first time I've complained about stuff being lost in the wash.) Unfortunately, I brought the same 6 socks out again about an hour later and couldn't understand why Jeanne blew her stack—until later she explained that I had repeated the action, which is what Alzheimer's disease is all about—unfortunately.

Was around WS house all morning. Jeanne paying bills and doing all the household bookkeeping/money-management as she has for several years—and I am delighted. She is better than I am at such duties—and I am getting continually less and less observant and my memory continues to fail. The net result is that Jeanne has become our comptroller/money manager, and "anchor to windward"—for which I thank God. I am lucky to have her. She does it all with no complaining or groaning and I hope she reads this someday!

The past 5 days are the first lapses in years of diary-keeping—other than when I was in Korea—and it is directly related to Alzheimer's disease, I believe. It is just plain difficult to remember!!! Anyway, this afternoon I worked on putting the electric davits back in operating condition, and tomorrow I expect to put that damn boat back in the water in operating condition after literally months of no use (just repairs/maintenance)!

Alzheimer's disease is pretty easy to detect! It won't be long before I'll have to give up this diary-keeping—after all these years—unless I can figure out a way of supplementing my "memory" with notes during the day.

Then, in December 1998, Budd Post wrote his final diary entry . . .

Date??? I don't know . . .

We had dinner downstairs at WS with Jim, Kerri, David, & Kelli—David & Kelli are in the green bedroom, Jim & Kerri and 3 kids downstairs. I am hopelessly confused—I don't know what day it is, or what date, but it is the new year, and we all had dinner together, and Jim & David & I fished in my boat~~~

Pure joy! Budd, Shannon, Devin & JD Post

Jeanne continues . . .

> *Toward the end, Budd didn't recognize me or Jimmy or his grandchildren. But, you know, he still talked about the Keys. He still remembered Waterside. That house and living in the Keys was what he wanted most out of life. It was his lifetime dream come true. And he never, ever forgot it.*
>
> *As Budd's Alzheimer's got worse and worse, I missed my husband. I missed the man he once was—the man who had such a great sense of humor—the man who could carry on a*

conversation better than anyone—the man who had been my companion and best friend for over fifty years. Even so, I loved him 'til the very end. I still love him.

Alzheimer's is such an awful disease. Fact is, there still isn't anything that can be done to prevent or cure it. My only hope is you will pray for new discoveries. I do.

14.

Always did. Always will.

Some flash lightning for a brief moment and are soon forgotten. Others leave a lasting, endearing glow. Through *A Man Named Budd,* Howard Malvern Post—Budd, with *two* Ds—will live forever.

Jimmy says . . .

> *Dad's story is a great story. These days, even though stories like his are sorely needed, there aren't many to be told. Dad's story has a positive influence on so many people, in South Florida and throughout the world.*
>
> *Over the years, PBS&J employed sixty thousand people and every single one was touched by Dad's vision—his quiet, yet present, leadership. Dad was an innovator—a spark plug. He was an expert delegator, but when things fell apart, he was the first one to pick you up and help you go again.*
>
> *There's a "joke" that every time someone worked for PBS&J at a VP or even managerial level,*

they left and started their own company, so Post, Buckley, Schuh and Jernigan was, actually, a "School of Engineering." It was the epitome of a privately owned corporation that was formed correctly, grew correctly, conducted itself correctly. It set the standards. There are literally hundreds, probably thousands, of successful engineering firms that were started by people who learned the correct way at PBS&J.

Jimmy and Budd. The first of many work days together.

Even today, almost forty years after Dad retired, I still meet people who say, "PBS&J was the best company, ever—and I don't mean just

engineering firm. Every day, I strive to run MY company the exact way your dad ran PBS&J."
PBS&J was a flawless machine.

Still, Dad was modest—a genuinely good, God-fearing man. But he never bragged. In part, that's because he was self-driven to be successful. In part, that's because of the values instilled by his parents. But, mainly, that's because of the pure pleasure he derived from the business. He enjoyed the hell out of it. He really did.

AND Dad was good. He could work a commission meeting, commissioners, and the public as smooth as silk. It was amazing to watch this otherwise quiet and shy man stand up, speak, and have everyone really listen.

Even though Dad helped create and build one of the finest engineering firms in the United States, he was a simple man at heart. He loved fishing, collecting driftwood, feeding great white herons, studying flora and fauna, enjoying wildlife. And then there was golf . . . golf was his ultimate passion, his obsession. And Waterside was his ultimate goal, his dream come true.

A Man Named Budd *preserves Dad's legacy. It is my way of honoring him. When he was still here, on this earth, I didn't tell him how much I loved him. That kills me. But here's my chance: Dad, you did all the right things. You taught me how to be successful in business, how to treat people, how to raise a kid, how to treat my wife, how to play golf.*

Yes, Dad, you taught me well. If I become half the man you were, I'll die a lucky man.

I love you, Dad.
Always did.
Always will.

References

Oradell, New Jersey

http://en.wikipedia.org/wiki/Oradell,_New_Jersey

https://picasaweb.google.com/oradellarchive/
OradellLocalHistoryArchivePhotos33

http://www.revolutionarywarnewjersey.com/
new_jersey_revolutionary_war_sites/towns/
oradell_nj_revolutionary_war_sites.htm

http://en.wikipedia.org/wiki/
American_Revolutionary_War

1920s

http://kclibrary.lonestar.edu/decade20.html

Model A Ford

http://www.shayhistory.com/HistoryFord.html

Great Depression

http://en.wikipedia.org/wiki/Wall_Street_Crash_of_1929

http://useconomy.about.com/od/glossary/g/Black-Thursday-1929.htm

http://useconomy.about.com/od/glossary/g/Black_Monday.htm

http://useconomy.about.com/od/glossary/g/Black_Tuesday.htm

Allapattah, Florida

http://sneakykitchen.com/forums/view_topic.php?id=236&forum_id=39

http://sneakykitchen.com/forums/view_topic.php?id=336&forum_id=39

http://sneakykitchen.com/forums/view_forum.php?id=39

Miami International Airport

http://golldiecat.tripod.com/history.html

Writing

http://en.wikipedia.org/wiki/Cuneiform

http://en.wikipedia.org/wiki/Sei_Sh%C5%8Dnagon

http://en.wikipedia.org/wiki/The_Pillow_Book

Boy Scouts of America

http://en.wikipedia.org/wiki/Boy_Scouts_of_America

http://www.scouting.org/meritbadges.aspx

http://en.wikipedia.org/wiki/
Ranks_in_the_Boy_Scouts_of_America

http://en.wikipedia.org/wiki/
Eagle_Scout_%28Boy_Scouts_of_America%29

http://www.boyscouttrail.com/content/ceremony/
eagle_feather-2139.asp

http://en.wikipedia.org/wiki/
Miami_Jackson_High_School

Military

Bible: John 5: 19-23

https://www.marionmilitary.edu/about/history.cms

http://history1900s.about.com/cs/worldwari/p/
lusitania.htm

http://history1900s.about.com/od/worldwari/p/World-War-I.htm

http://history1900s.about.com/od/worldwari/a/
Zimmermann-Telegram.htm

http://www.campblanding-museum.org/history.html

http://www.campfannin.org/history.aspx

http://www.tshaonline.org/handbook/online/articles/qbc20

http://en.wikipedia.org/wiki/Fort_Benning

http://www.georgiaencyclopedia.org/articles/
government-politics/fort-benning

http://en.wikipedia.org/wiki/
United_States_Army_Reserve

http://en.wikipedia.org/wiki/Korean_War

http://www.history.com/topics/korean-war

http://www.usar.army.mil/ourstory/Pages/default.aspx

http://www.history.com/topics/cold-war/dean-acheson

Golf

http://inventors.about.com/od/gstartinventions/a/
golf_2.htm

http://en.wikipedia.org/wiki/History_of_golf

http://www.seattlepi.com/sports/article/Sports-
Beat-1192437.php

http://dictionary.reference.com/browse/golf?s=t

http://www.electricscotland.com/history/other/rattray_john.htm

http://www.saintandrewsgolfclub.com/public/history.aspx

http://en.wikipedia.org/wiki/Gutta-percha

http://www.brainyquote.com/quotes/quotes/m/marktwain100019.html

PBS&J

PBS&J Company Profile

Articles of Incorporation the PBS&J Corporation

http://www.pbsj.com

Wilkinson, Jerry. History of the Card Sound Community

http://www.fla-keys.com/roadwork.cfm

Environment

http://www.monroecounty-fl.gov/DocumentCenter/Home/View/1290

http://www.tampabay.com/news/environment/wildlife/no-jolly-disney-ending-for-endangered-key-largo-wood-rats-bred-at-animal/1239400

http://pennekamppark.com/history/

http://www.fla-keys.com/news/news.cfm?sid=7944

Proposed Carysfort Lighthouse Offshore Marine Research Facility, Repairs and Rehabilitation Plans prepared for Pennekamp Coral Reef Institute, Inc. by Post, Buckley, Schuh & Jernigan, Inc. (no date).

Letter dated February 25, 1994 to The Honorable Peter Deutsch, from Alison Farher, President Pennekamp Coral Reef Institute, Inc.

http://www.dep.state.fl.us/coastal/habitats/coral/

Anti-Castro Movement

http://en.wikipedia.org/wiki/Fidel_Castro

http://www.jfklibrary.org/JFK/JFK-in-History/The-Bay-of-Pigs.aspx

http://news.google.com/newspapers?nid=1298&dat=19640512&id=-dhNAAAAIBAJ&sjid=w4oDAAAAIBAJ&pg=1523,3685875

http://www.ploughshares.org/blog/2012-10-15/cuban-missile-crisis-five-things

Alzheimer's disease

http://www.caregiver.com/channels/alz/
articles/a_brief_history.htm

http://www.about-alzheimers.com/history-of-alzheimers.
shtml

About the Author

Judith Kolva, Ph.D., founder and CEO of Legacies In Ink, LLC, is a professional personal historian, with a doctoral degree in the psychology and practice of personal history. She travels internationally to preserve stories of individuals, families, and businesses. Judith lives in Fort Lauderdale, Florida with her husband and business partner, Charles J. Schwabe. Learn more at LegaciesInk.com